Fabulous Fashions

May God Bless You
Martha Pullen

To Angie
May God Bless You
Martha Pullen
8-24-04

Martha Pullen Company, Inc.
149 Old Big Cove Road · Brownsboro, AL 35741 · Phone: 256.533.9586 · Fax: 256.533.9630
info@marthapullen.com · www.marthapullen.com

D1003185

Introduction

Just how did this book originate? I would love to share the story. For ten years we have produced Martha's Sewing Room, a television series for PBS stations across the country. I am thrilled that at last report our series airs in approximately 57% of all PBS stations in the United States. We air in many places in Canada and 13 shows have been translated into Japanese. I wanted clothing which would be beautiful on me as well as on my twenty seven year old daughter, Joanna who is modeling with me on the cover. I think Martha's Fabulous Fashions are truly beautiful clothes and I love wearing mine.

Every year we have to make decisions for the theme and patterns for the year. We always have several quilts, doll dresses, home decorating projects, Sew Kool 4 Kids projects and of course the attic antiqué clothing which is already prepared since the garments are from my personal collection which I have been accumulating for over 25 years. Joe says I have an unnatural attraction to antiqué white clothes. Sometimes men just don't understand collections such as antiqué clothing and fabric, do they?

For this very special TV year, our tenth, we decided that women truly are wanting to sew more for themselves and many times cannot find patterns which they like and which show them how to use these fabulous machine embroidery features which some people have. Some people just want a beautiful outfit with no machine embroidery at all. Many people need large sizes and I might add many people need very small sizes. Presenting easy to wear clothing for women of all sizes has become a specialty here at Martha Pullen Company. If you want my true confessions, I love to have patterns available which make mature figures look beautiful no matter if the maturity is very thin or a little fluffy.

An earlier book, Six Easy Patterns for Women Only (featured on our TV series several years ago) is still a runaway best seller. The clothes are very figure flattering and give tons of ideas for using our beloved embroidery machines and sergers. Since women around the world loved our clothing in that book and actually started sewing for themselves again, we began to realize that our style of women's fashions were universally appealing.

What I am trying to get to is finally our decision was made to have another women's book featuring patterns which are beautiful, stylish, multi-sized (lots of sizes) and which showcase machine embroidery and other features available on sewing machines. We also have a touch of handwork with Beverley Sheldrick's two outfits and her lovely silk ribbon embroidery segments on our series.

I chose a lovely loose fitting jacket with a simple sleeveless dress to go underneath the jacket. The jacket in Martha's Fabulous Fashions is simply an artist's palette for machine work as well as for handwork, if that is your favorite. Originally, I planned this dress and jacket for very drapey fabrics such as rayon, cotton netting, silk organza, polyester, and knits.

When my brown dress arrived with the Zundt lace embroidery designs on the cotton netting as well a rayon lace and antique lace--all dyed a beautiful medium brown, I simply thought that was the most beautiful dress that I had ever put on. I wore it to my niece Anna's wedding received so many compliments on the outfit. Our designers loved these ideas but also wanted to create the outfits in linen and silk dupioni. The results are spectacular in both types of fabrics. As a matter of fact, in the more crisp fabrics such as linen and silk dupioni, the fronts of the jacket overlap in an asymmetrical way when they are closed. On the drapey fabrics, the fronts of the jacket just fall straight.

We needed two more pieces for the book and I always love over blouses which are loose and comfortable. I love skirts with elastic waists when they are going to be covered up with an over blouse. To be truthful, I don't own a skirt or pair of pants which does not have an elastic waistline. They are so comfortable! I also don't tuck in shirts so the elastic does not show. This over blouse is so cute with its pockets in the front and the back casing to pull up the fullness to your desired fit. The straight skirt has two back opening treatments and once again is a very flattering skirt.

We have given ways to cut off the dress to make a cropped top or shell. This variation is in addition to the four original patterns. I do hope you enjoy making some of the garments this book. One thing is for sure, we have included sizes for almost everyone that you love to sew for. Please enjoy making these garments for yourself. In deciding which size is best for you, please either make up a quick muslin or flat pattern measure a loose fitting jacket you already have and compare the patterns. We have given a measurement chart developed by our pattern drafters. Some people like clothing more fitted; some like it loose. These clothes are not closely fitted as you can see; however, you can still choose the degree of "looseness" which best suits your taste. Please enjoy these patterns as much as we have enjoyed bringing them to you. I would like to thank all of the designers who made the garments and who traveled to the studios to present their garment on our shows. I would also like to thank all of the PBS stations around the country (and the world) who air Martha's Sewing Room. But most of all, I would like to thank you, our loyal customers, who continue to love our patterns, books, TV series, educational events, magazine (Sew Beautiful) and who are so loyal to us. To God be the glory, great things He has done.

BOOK TEAM

EDITOR-IN-CHIEF
Martha Campbell Pullen, Ph.D.

BOOK DESIGN AND LAYOUT
Jamie W. Robinson

PHOTOGRAPHY
Jennifer & Company

STYLIST
Claudia Newton

ILLUSTRATIONS
Angela Cataldo Pullen, Kris Broom,
Charlotte Potter

EDITORIAL DIRECTOR
Charlotte Potter

CONSTRUCTION CONSULTANTS AND
WRITERS
Martha Pullen, Charlotte Potter,
Claudia Newton, Patty Smith,
Kathy McMakin

PROJECT DESIGNERS
Marlis Bennett, Peggy Dilbone,
Pam Mahshie, Connie Palmer,
Beverley Sheldrick, Patty Smith,
Sue Pennington Stewart,
Diane Witt

PRODUCTION MANAGER
Leighann Lott

Martha Pullen Company, Inc.
149 Old Big Cove Road
Brownsboro, AL 35741

Phone: 256.533.9586
Fax: 256.533.9630

www.marthapullen.com
info@marthapullen.com

ISBN: 1-878048-36-8

Table of Contents

Front Cover: Zündt Embroidered Jacket and Dress (left) and Cornelli Lace Jacket and Dress (right)

Dress/Top General Directions

Basic Dress

Basic Top

Pattern Pieces
(located on the pattern tissue)
- Dress/Top Front
- Dress/Top Back

Cutting and Preparing the Pieces
Refer to the layout guide on the pattern tissue sheets and cut the following:
- One front on the fold - remove the 5/8″ seam allowance from the neck edge and armhole edges after cutting (**fig. 1**) and mark the darts in the dress/top front
- Two backs - remove the 5/8″ seam allowance from the neck edge and armhole edges after cutting (**fig. 2**)
- Bias strips 1-1/2″ wide to go around the neck and the two armholes

Supplies
- Fabric for Dress

Size	45″ with/without nap	60″ with/without nap
XS	3-1/4 yards	2 yards
SM	3-1/4 yards	2-1/4 yards
MD	3-3/8 yards	2-1/2 yards
LG – XL	3-3/8 yards	3-1/8 yards
2XL	3-3/8 yards	3-3/8 yards
3XL	4 yards	3-3/8 yards
4XL	4-3/8 yards	3-3/8 yards

- Fabric for Top

Size	45″ with/without nap	60″ with/without nap
XS	1-1/4 yards	1-1/4 yards
SM-LG	1-5/8 yards	1-1/4 yards
XL-2XL	1-3/4 yards	1-1/4 yards
3XL-4XL	1-7/8 yards	1-7/8 yards

- Thread to match the fabric
- Basic sewing supplies

Front

Remove seam allowances

Figure 1

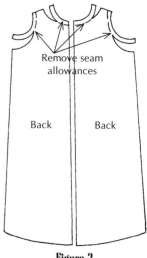

Remove seam allowances

Back   Back

Figure 2

Dress/Top General Construction

All seams are 5/8" unless otherwise noted. To finish the seams, trim the seams to 1/4" and overcast the edges by machine or serger.

1. Stitch the bias strips together to make one continuous length of bias (**fig. 3**). Fold the bias in half lengthwise, matching the raw edges; press a crease, being careful not to stretch the bias.

2. Optional: Stitch the darts in the dress/top front (**fig. 4**). Press the darts toward the bottom of the dress/top.

3. With right sides together stitch the center back seam of the dress/top (**fig. 5**). Finish the seam and press to one side.

4. With right sides together stitch the shoulder seams (**fig. 6**). Finish the seams and press toward the back.

5. Pin the bias strip to the neck edge with right sides together, beginning at the center back with the end folded back; match the raw edges of the bias tape to the raw edge of the dress/top neck edge (**fig. 7**). When the bias has been pinned around the neck edge, allow the end of the bias to overlap the beginning by approximately 1/2" (**fig. 8**). Trim away any excess bias.

6. Stitch the bias to the neck edge with a 1/4" seam allowance. (**fig. 8**). Clip the seam allowance. Press the bias and the seam allowance away from the garment.

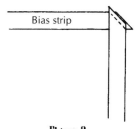

Figure 3

Bias strip

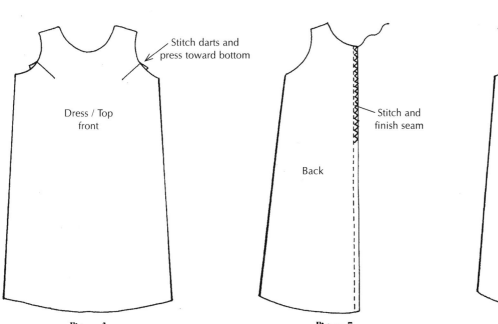

Stitch darts and press toward bottom

Dress / Top front

Figure 4

Stitch and finish seam

Back

Figure 5

Stitch and finish shoulders

Front

Figure 6

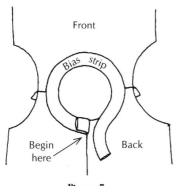

Front

Bias strip

Begin here

Back

Figure 7

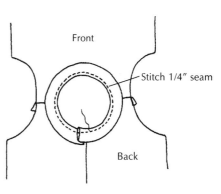

Front

Stitch 1/4" seam

Back

Figure 8

7. Finish the bias neckline by hand or machine as follows:

Hand
- Wrap the bias over the seam allowance and allow the fold of the bias to meet the stitching line on the wrong side of the dress/top. Stitch the fold in place by hand (**fig. 9**).

Machine
- Trim the seam allowance slightly narrower than 1/4". Wrap the bias over the seam allowance and allow the fold of the bias to fall just beyond the stitching line on the wrong side of the dress/top. From the right side of the dress/top, machine stitch "in the ditch," catching the fold of the bias in the stitching (**fig. 10**).

8. Stitch the bias tape to the armhole edges with a 1/4" seam allowance. (**fig. 11**). Clip the seam allowance. Press the bias binding and the seam allowance away from the garment.

9. Stitch the side seams (**fig. 12**) and press the seams toward the dress/top back. Finish the bias, referring to step 7 above.

10. Hem the bottom of the dress/top by pressing 1/4" to the wrong side. Then turn up another 3/8" and straight stitch in place (**fig. 13**).

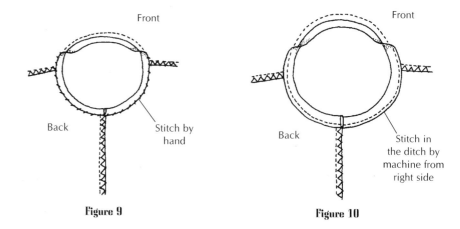

Front

Back

Stitch by hand

Figure 9

Front

Back

Stitch in the ditch by machine from right side

Figure 10

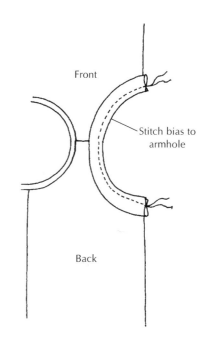

Front

Stitch bias to armhole

Back

Figure 11

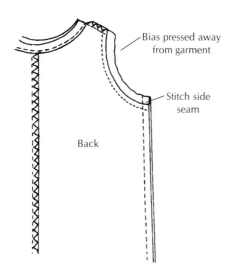

Bias pressed away from garment

Stitch side seam

Back

Figure 12

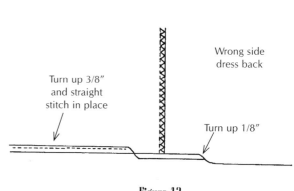

Turn up 3/8" and straight stitch in place

Wrong side dress back

Turn up 1/8"

Figure 13

Jacket General Directions

Back view

Supplies

- Fabric

Size	Main Fabric 45" w/wo nap	Main Fabric 60" w/wo nap	Contrast Fabric 45" w/wo nap	Contrast Fabric 60" w/wo nap
XS-MD	2-1/8 yards	1-5/8 yards	7/8 yard	3/4 yard
LG	2-1/4 yards	1-5/8 yards	7/8 yard	3/4 yard
XL	2-3/8 yards	1-5/8 yards	1-1/8 yards	7/8 yard
2XL	2-3/8 yards	2 yards	1-1/8 yards	7/8 yard
3XL	2-5/8 yards	2 yards	1-1/8 yards	7/8 yard
4XL	2-5/8 yards	2-1/8 yards	1-1/8 yards	7/8 yard

NOTE: For the lined jacket, purchase lining in the amount listed above for main fabric. For the unlined version of the jacket with the bias binding, an additional 1/3 yards of fabric will be needed for making bias. Or purchase 2-1/3 yards of 1/4" double-fold bias tape to match the garment. Follow the instructions included with the bias tape for applying it to the jacket.

- 1-1/3 yards of purchased or self-made cording for the jacket ties
- Thread to match fabrics
- Basic sewing supplies

Pattern Pieces

(located on the pattern tissue)

- Jacket Upper Front
- Jacket Lower Front
- Jacket Lower Front Overlay
- Jacket Back
- Jacket Side Back
- Jacket Upper Sleeve
- Jacket Lower Sleeve
- Jacket Shoulder to Tie Neck Ruffle or Jacket Shoulder to Hem Neck Ruffle

Template

(located on the pattern tissue)

- Curve for ruffle Front (optional)

Cutting the Pieces

Refer to the layout guide on the pattern tissue sheets and cut the following pieces from the main fabric:

- Two jacket upper fronts
- Two jacket lower fronts
- One jacket back on the fold
- Two jacket side backs
- Two jacket upper sleeves

Refer to the layout guide on the pattern tissue sheets and cut the following pieces from the contrast fabric:

- Two jacket lower front overlays
- Two jacket lower sleeves
- Two jacket shoulder-to-tie neck ruffles

For the unlined jacket, cut the following pieces from the main fabric:

- Bias strips 1-3/4" wide to go around the neckline and down the center front of the jacket

For the lined jacket, cut these pieces from the lining fabric:

- Two jacket upper fronts
- Two jacket lower fronts
- One jacket back on the fold
- Two jacket side backs
- Two jacket upper sleeves

Jacket General Construction

All seams are 5/8" unless otherwise noted. To finish the seams, trim the seams to 1/4" and overcast the edges by machine or serger.

1. Finish the curved edge of the lower front overlay with a rolled hem on a serger or by using a rolled hem foot on the sewing machine (**fig. 1**).

2. Place the lower front overlay on top of the jacket lower front and pin in place. Straight stitch 1/2" from the top and side edges to secure the two pieces together (**fig. 2**). They will now be treated as one piece.

3. Stitch a line of lengthened straight stitching for easing across the upper edge of the jacket lower front (**fig. 3**).

4. Place the jacket upper front to the jacket lower front with right sides together; stitch the seam, easing the edge of the jacket lower front to fit the jacket upper front (**fig. 4**).

5. Repeat steps 1 through 4 for the other side of the jacket front. Press the seams down.

6. Place the jacket side back to one side of the jacket back, right sides together. Stitch, clip and finish the seam. Press the seam toward the jacket back (**fig. 5**).

7. Repeat step 6 for the remaining jacket side back. Press the seams toward the center back (**fig. 5**).

8. Place the jacket front to the jacket back, right sides together, matching the shoulder and side seams. Stitch and finish the seams; press the seams toward the back (**fig. 6**).

9. Finish the outside edges of the neck ruffles with a rolled hem on a serger or by using a rolled hem foot on the sewing machine (**fig. 7**).

10. Stay stitch 5/8" from the inside neck edge of each ruffle. Clip to the stay stitching at regular intervals around the inner circle to open out the ruffle (**fig. 7**). Lay the jacket and the neck ruffles aside.

11. Finish the bottom edge of the lower sleeve in the same manner as the outside edge of the neck ruffles (**fig. 8**).

12. Place the lower sleeve to the upper sleeve, right sides together. Stitch and finish the seam. Press the seam toward the upper sleeve (**fig. 9**).

13. Fold the sleeve with right sides together; stitch and finish the seam. Press the seam toward the front (**fig. 10a**). Optional: Turn up a 5/8" hem in the lower sleeve and stitch by hand or machine (**fig. 10b**).

* Complete either the Unlined Jacket Version steps or the Lined Jacket Version steps to finish the jacket.

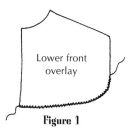

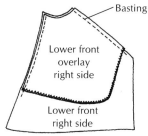

Lower front overlay

Figure 1

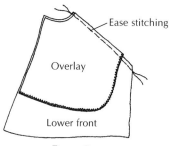

Basting

Lower front overlay right side

Lower front right side

Figure 2

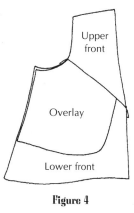

Ease stitching

Overlay

Lower front

Figure 3

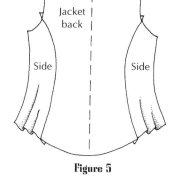

Upper front

Overlay

Lower front

Figure 4

Jacket back

Side   Side

Figure 5

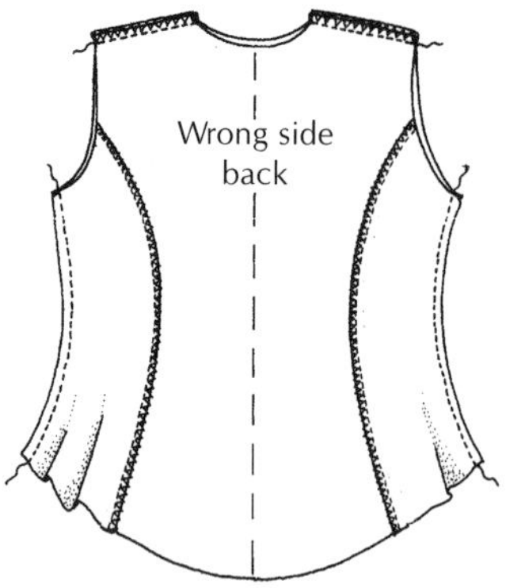

Wrong side back

Figure 6

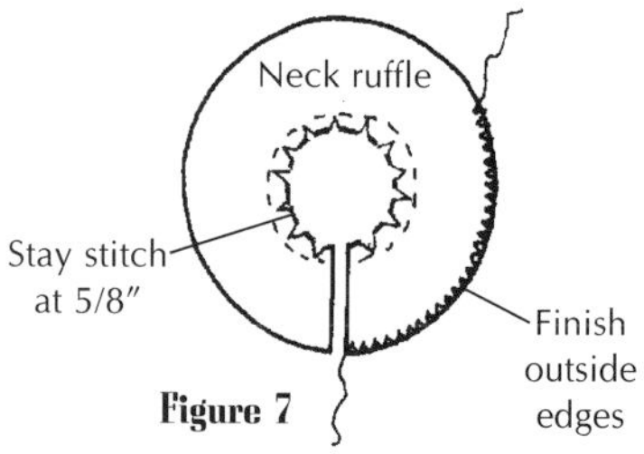

Neck ruffle

Stay stitch at 5/8"

Finish outside edges

Figure 7

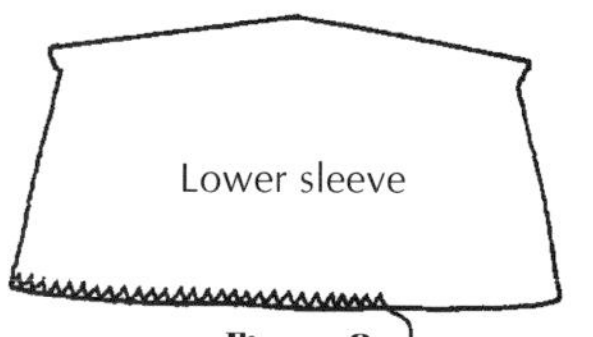

Lower sleeve

Figure 8

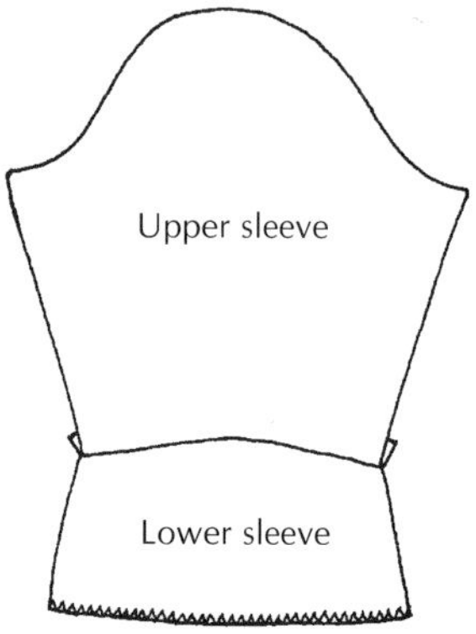

Upper sleeve

Lower sleeve

Figure 9

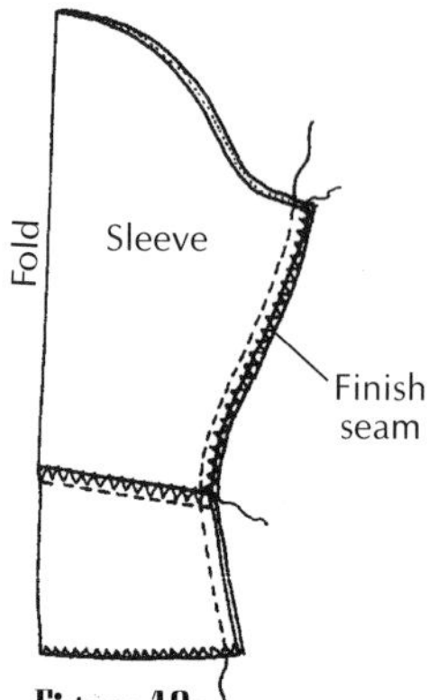

Fold

Sleeve

Finish seam

Figure 10a

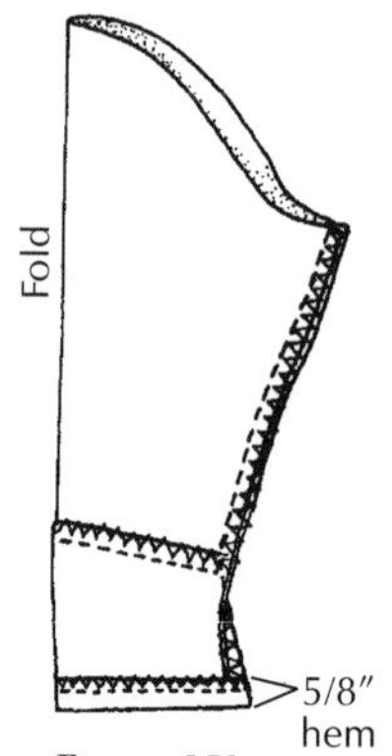

Fold

5/8" hem

Figure 10b

Unlined Jacket Version

(Neckline and jacket front are finished with a 1/4″ bias binding)

1. Remove the 5/8″ seam allowance from the neck edge and down the front of the jacket (**fig. 11**).

2. Finish the lower raw edge of the jacket hemline with a zigzag or serge (**fig. 11**). Fold 5/8″ to the inside to form the jacket hem and press (**fig. 12**). Hem the jacket by machine or hand.

3. Stitch the bias strips together to make one continuous length of bias (**fig. 13**).

4. Press the strips in half lengthwise being very careful not to stretch the bias (**fig. 14**).

5. Trim 5/8″ from the inside neck edge of the neck ruffles, trimming along the previously stitched line (**fig. 15a**). Stay stitch 1/4″ from the cut edge and clip to the stay stitching (**fig. 15b**). Pin the wrong side of the neck ruffles to the right side of the jacket from the shoulder seam to the center front neckline. Stitch the ruffles to the jacket at a scant 1/4″ from the raw edges (**fig. 15c**). The ruffles and jacket will now be treated as one.

6. Pin the folded bias to the jacket neck edge and down the front edge of the jacket, matching the raw edges. Allow approximately 1/2″ to extend at the lower edge of the jacket.

7. Stitch the bias to the jacket 1/4″ from the raw edges (**fig. 16**).

8. Finish the bias by hand or machine as follows:

   Hand
   - Fold up the 1/2″ bias extension. Wrap the bias over the seam allowance and allow the fold of the bias to meet the stitching line on the wrong side of the jacket. Stitch the fold in place by hand (**fig. 17**).

   Machine
   - Trim the seam allowance slightly narrower than 1/4″. Fold up the 1/2″ bias extension. Wrap the bias over the seam allowance and allow the fold of the bias to fall just beyond the stitching line on the wrong side of the jacket (**fig. 18**).

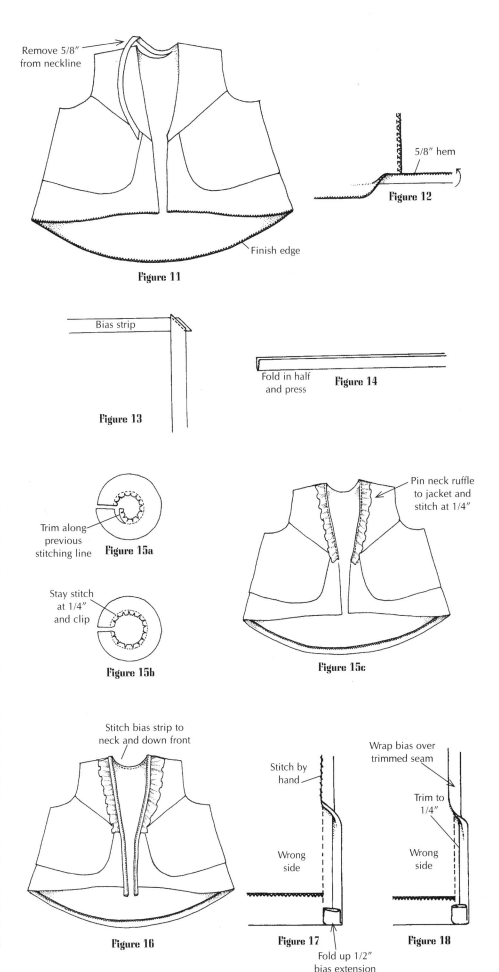

Remove 5/8″ from neckline

Figure 11

Finish edge

5/8″ hem

Figure 12

Bias strip

Figure 13

Fold in half and press   Figure 14

Trim along previous stitching line   Figure 15a

Stay stitch at 1/4″ and clip   Figure 15b

Pin neck ruffle to jacket and stitch at 1/4″

Figure 15c

Stitch bias strip to neck and down front

Figure 16

Stitch by hand

Wrong side

Fold up 1/2″ bias extension

Figure 17

Wrap bias over trimmed seam

Trim to 1/4″

Wrong side

Figure 18

From the right side of the jacket, machine stitch "in the ditch," catching the fold of the bias in the stitching (**fig. 19**).

9. Stitch a row of lengthened machine stitching between the notches on the sleeve cap for easing (**fig. 20**). Pin the sleeves into the armholes, matching the notches and the side seams of the jacket to the sleeve seams. Stitch and finish the seams (**fig. 21**). Press the seams toward the sleeves.

10. Cut the cording into two 24" pieces. Attach the cords on the inside of the jacket (**fig. 22**).

Lined Jacket Version

1. Finish the lower raw edge of the jacket hemline with a zigzag or serge (**see fig. 11**). Fold 5/8" to the inside to form the jacket hem and press (**see fig. 12**). Hem the jacket by machine or hand.

2. Pin the wrong side of the neck ruffles to the right side of the jacket from the shoulder seam to the center front neckline. Stitch the ruffles to the jacket at the 5/8" seam lines (**see fig. 15**). The ruffles and jacket will now be treated as one.

3. Follow steps 3 through 8 and step 12 in General Construction and construct the jacket lining. Finish the lower edge of the jacket lining with a zigzag or serge. Turn up a 3/4" hem along the bottom edge of the jacket lining and press (**refer to fig. 12**).

4. Fold the sleeve lining with right sides together; stitch and finish the seam. Press the seam toward the front (**refer to fig. 10a**).

5. Slip the sleeve lining into the sleeve with the wrong side of the lining to the wrong side of the sleeve, matching the seams and aligning the top edges of the sleeve caps. Baste the layers together along sleeve caps (**fig. 23**).

6. Turn under 5/8" at the lower edge of the upper sleeve lining and stitch the folded edge to the seam allowance by hand or machine (**fig. 24**).

7. Cut the cording into two 24" pieces. Attach the cords on the right side of the jacket so they will be caught in the seam allowance (**fig. 25**)

8. Place the jacket and the jacket lining right sides together and stitch around the neckline and down the center front, catching the cording in the stitching (**fig. 26**). Reinforce the stitching at the cord. Clip the curves and points.

9. Turn the lining to the inside of the jacket and press well. Pull the ruffle out of the way and topstitch through the jacket and lining approximately 1/8" from the finished edge of the jacket. The stitching will fall underneath the ruffles (**fig. 27**).

10. Pin the jacket lining to the jacket at the armholes and baste in place (**fig. 27**). Stitch a row of lengthened machine stitching between the notches on the sleeve cap for easing (**fig. 28**).

11. Pin the sleeves into the armholes, matching the side seams of the jacket to the sleeve seams and matching the notches. Stitch and finish the seams (**refer to fig. 21**).

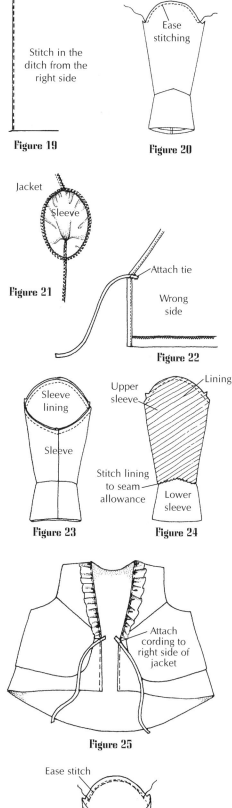

Stitch in the ditch from the right side

Figure 19

Ease stitching

Figure 20

Jacket
Sleeve

Figure 21

Attach tie

Wrong side

Figure 22

Sleeve lining

Sleeve

Figure 23

Upper sleeve

Lining

Stitch lining to seam allowance

Lower sleeve

Figure 24

Attach cording to right side of jacket

Figure 25

Ease stitch

Figure 28

Stitch jacket to lining around neck and down center front

Lining wrong side

Figure 26

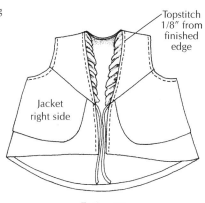

Topstitch 1/8" from finished edge

Jacket right side

Figure 27

Martha's Fabulous Fashions

Over Blouse General Directions

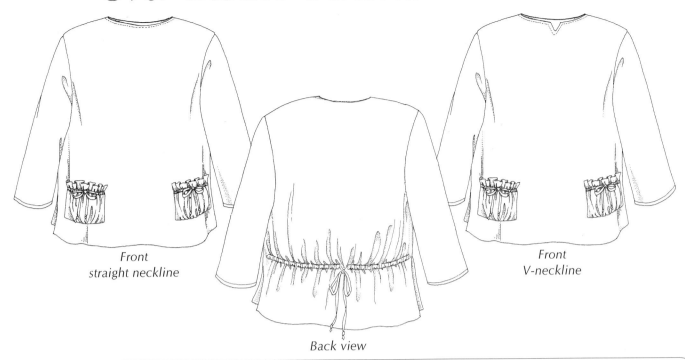

Front
straight neckline

Back view

Front
V-neckline

Supplies

- Fabric

Size	Main Fabric 45″ w/wo nap	Main Fabric 60″ w/wo nap	Contrast Fabric* 45″ w/wo nap	Contrast Fabric* 60″ w/wo nap
XS	2-3/4 yards	1-7/8 yards	3/8 yard	3/8 yard
SM-MD	2-7/8 yards	2-1/8 yards	3/8 yard	3/8 yard
LG	3 yards	2-1/8 yards	3/8 yard	3/8 yard
XL	3 yards	2-1/8 yards	3/8 yard	3/8 yard
2XL-3XL	3-1/8 yards	2-3/4 yards	3/8 yard	3/8 yard
4XL	3-1/8 yards	2-7/8 yards	3/8 yard	3/8 yard

* Contrast fabric may be purchased for the pieces listed below. Or you may wish to purchase additional main fabric (yardage given under the contrast fabric heading) so that all pieces are cut from the same fabric.

- 1/4 yard of 45″ wide interfacing suitable for the chosen fabric
- Thread to match the fabric
- Basic sewing supplies

Pattern Pieces

(located on the pattern tissue)

- Over Blouse Front with or without V (curved hem or straight hem version)
- Over Blouse Front Facing
- Over Blouse Back (curved hem or straight hem version)
- Over Blouse Back Facing
- Over Blouse Sleeve
- Over Blouse Sleeve Wrist Binding
- Over Blouse Pocket
- Over Blouse Back Tie Casing
- Over Blouse Back Tie
- Over Blouse Pocket Tie

Cutting and Preparing the Pieces

Refer to the layout guide on the tissue sheet and cut the following from the main fabric:

- One over blouse front on the fold - mark the pocket placements, armhole notches and side notch
- One over blouse back on the fold - mark the casing placement (re-position the casing placement lines as needed to fit), armhole notches, and side notch
- One over blouse front facing on the fold
- One over blouse back facing on the fold
- Two over blouse sleeves - mark the notches and shoulder dot
- Two over blouse pockets - mark the fold line, casing position lines and buttonhole placements
- One over blouse back tie casing - mark the buttonhole placements

Refer to the layout guide on the tissue sheet and cut the following from the contrast fabric:

- Two over blouse back ties
- Four over blouse pocket ties
- Two over blouse sleeve wrist bindings

*Re-position the casing placement lines as need to fit.

Cut the following from interfacing:

- One over blouse front facing on the fold
- One over blouse back facing on the fold

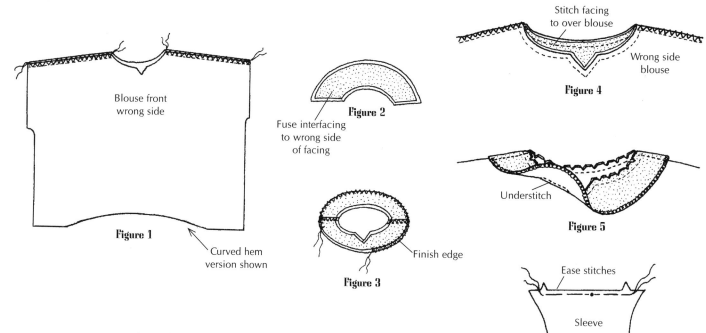

Blouse front wrong side

Figure 1

Curved hem version shown

Figure 2

Fuse interfacing to wrong side of facing

Figure 3

Finish edge

Figure 4

Stitch facing to over blouse

Wrong side blouse

Figure 5

Understitch

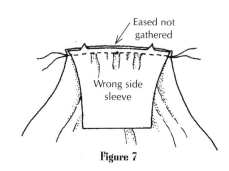

Ease stitches

Sleeve

Figure 6

Over Blouse General Construction

All seams are 5/8" unless otherwise noted. To finish the seam, trim the seam to 1/4" and overcast the edge by machine or serger.

1. Place the over blouse front and the over blouse back with right sides together, matching the shoulder seams. Stitch the shoulder seams. Finish the seams, and press the seams toward the over blouse back (**fig. 1**).

2. Trim 1/2" from all sides of the interfacing. Fuse (or adhere with temporary spray adhesive) the facing interfacings to the wrong side of the facings. The interfacing/facing unit will now be treated as one piece (**fig. 2**). Place the over blouse front facing and the over blouse back facing with right sides together. Stitch the shoulder seams of the facings. Finish the seams and lower edge of the facing with a zigzag or serger (**fig. 3**).

3. Place the facing to the over blouse neckline with right sides together, matching the shoulder seams.

4. Stitch the facing to the over blouse along the neckline (**fig. 4**). Trim and clip the seam allowances and points. Press the facing away from the garment and understitch the neck facing, stitching only through the seam allowance and the facing (**fig. 5**). Turn the facing to the wrong side. Hand tack the facing to the over blouse at the shoulder seams.

5. Stitch a row of lengthened machine stitching between the notches on the sleeve for easing (**fig. 6**). Match the notches on the top edge of the sleeve to the notches on the over blouse. Also, match the dot on the sleeve to the shoulder seam. Stitch the sleeve to the over blouse (**fig. 7**). Finish the seam. Press the seam allowance toward the over blouse.

6. Place the sleeve wrist binding to the lower edge of each sleeve with right sides together and raw edges even. Stitch with a 5/8" seam allowance (**fig. 8**). Press the seam allowance toward the binding.

7. Place stabilizer on the wrong side of the back casing under the buttonhole marks. Stitch two 1/2" buttonholes at the placement markings in the center of the over blouse back tie casing (**fig. 9**). Remove the stabilizer. Cut the buttonholes open.

8. Turn under 1/4" along each long edge of the back tie casing and press (**fig. 10**).

9. Position the casing onto the right side of the over blouse back along the casing position guidelines.

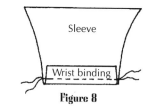

Eased not gathered

Wrong side sleeve

Figure 7

Sleeve

Wrist binding

Figure 8

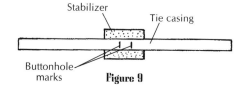

Stabilizer

Tie casing

Buttonhole marks

Figure 9

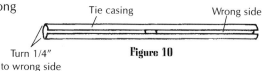

Tie casing

Wrong side

Turn 1/4" to wrong side

Figure 10

10. Topstitch the casing very close to each long edge. Do not stitch across the ends of the casing at the side seams (**fig. 11**).
11. Fold the two over blouse back ties in half lengthwise and stitch along the long edges and across one end. Clip the corners (**fig. 12**), turn right side out and press.
12. With a large safety pin or bodkin, run the ties through the casing; place the seam edges of the ties down and match the remaining raw edges of the ties with the side edges of the over blouse back. Pin the raw edges of the tie to the over blouse at the opening of the casing. The finished ends of the ties will exit the buttonholes at the center of the casing (**fig. 13**).

   * *If pockets are desired, refer to the instructions for Pockets at the end of these instructions and complete the steps.*

13. With right sides together, match the front to the back at the edge of the sleeve binding, the underarm seam and the bottom edge of the over blouse. Stitch the sleeve and side seams of the over blouse, beginning at the sleeve binding and stopping at the notch just below the back casing. Backstitch at the notch to secure. This will create a vent on each side of the over blouse (**fig. 14**).
14. Clip through the seam allowance on each side of the over blouse at the point where the stitching stops. Finish the side seam from the clip to the edge of the sleeve binding (**fig. 14**).
15. Finish the raw edges of the fabric on each side of the vents with a zigzag or serge (**fig. 15**).
16. Finish the lower edge of the front and back with a zigzag or serge (**fig. 15**).
17. Turn up a 3/8″ hem along the lower edge of the over blouse and pin in place (**fig. 16**).
18. At each vent, fold 5/8″ to the wrong side and press along each edge.
19. Topstitch the hem 1/4″ from the fold and the vents 1/2″ from the fold in one continuous topstitching line (**fig. 17**).

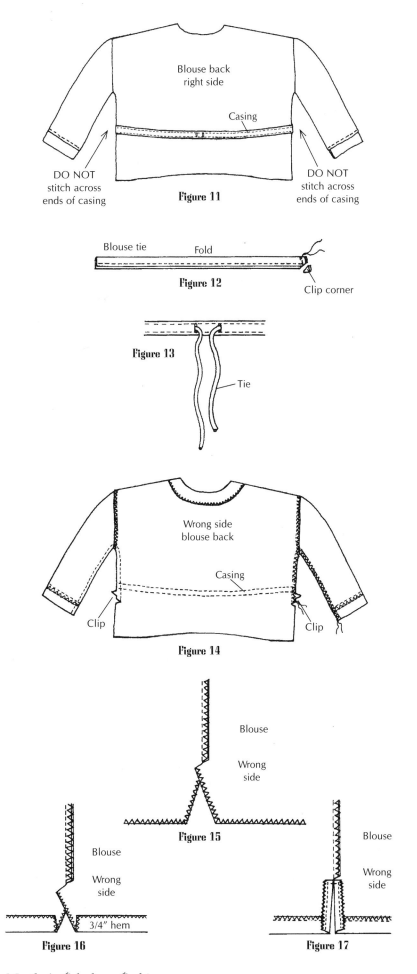

Blouse back
right side

Casing

DO NOT
stitch across
ends of casing

DO NOT
stitch across
ends of casing

Figure 11

Blouse tie   Fold

Figure 12

Clip corner

Figure 13

Tie

Wrong side
blouse back

Casing

Clip   Clip

Figure 14

Blouse

Wrong
side

Figure 15

Blouse

Wrong
side

3/4″ hem

Figure 16

Blouse

Wrong
side

Figure 17

20. Fold under 5/8″ along the unfinished long edge of each sleeve binding and press (**fig. 18**).
21. Fold the sleeve binding to the wrong side to meet the previous stitching. Stitch in place by hand or machine (**fig. 19**).
22. Pull up the back ties and tie into a bow at the center of the over blouse back.

Pockets

1. Finish all four edges of one pocket with a zigzag or serge (**fig. 20**).
2. Place stabilizer on the wrong side of the pocket under the buttonhole marks. Work two 1/2″ buttonholes on the pocket at the placement marks (**refer to fig. 9**). Cut the buttonholes open. Remove the excess stabilizer.
3. Fold the top edge of the pocket to the inside along the fold line and press.
4. Create a casing by stitching along the casing position lines (**fig. 21**).
5. Fold the two pocket ties in half lengthwise and stitch along the long edges and the angled edge with a 1/4″ seam (**refer to fig. 12**). Clip the corners and turn the ties right side out. Press well.
6. With a large safety pin or bodkin, run the ties through the pocket casing; place the seam edges of the ties down and match the remaining raw edges of the ties with the side edges of the pocket. The angled ends of the ties will exit the buttonholes at the center of the pocket (**fig. 22**).
7. Turn under 5/8″ along each side and the lower edge of the pocket and press in place (**fig. 23**).
8. Position the pocket onto the over blouse front along the marked placement lines (see finished drawing). Note that the pocket will appear too full in the center. The fullness will be gathered up by the ties running through the casing.
9. Straight stitch very close to the bottom and side edges of the pocket, securing it to the over blouse (**fig. 24**).
10. Stitch a small triangle at the top corners of the pocket to reinforce the pocket (**fig. 25**).
11. Repeat steps 1 through 10 for the other pocket.
12. Pull up the pocket ties and tie into a bow.

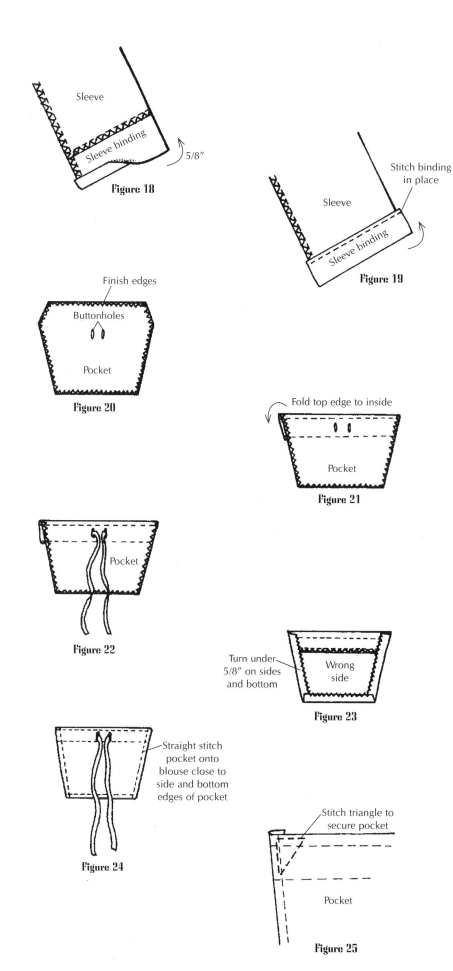

Figure 18

Figure 19

Finish edges
Buttonholes
Pocket
Figure 20

Fold top edge to inside
Pocket
Figure 21

Pocket
Figure 22

Turn under 5/8″ on sides and bottom
Wrong side
Figure 23

Straight stitch pocket onto blouse close to side and bottom edges of pocket
Figure 24

Stitch triangle to secure pocket
Pocket
Figure 25

Skirt General Directions

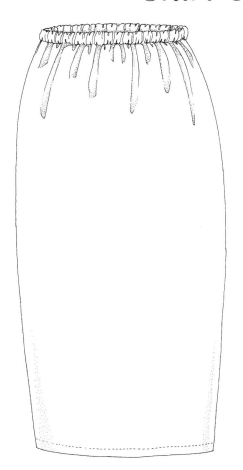

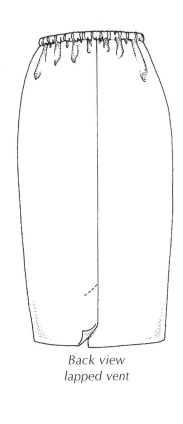

Back view
lapped vent

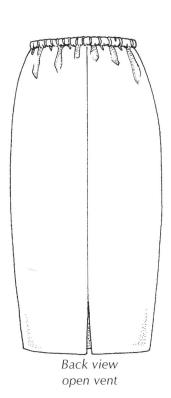

Back view
open vent

Supplies

- Fabric

Size	45" with/without nap	60" with/without nap
XS-XL	2-1/2 yards	1-3/8 yards
2XL	2-1/2 yards	2 yards
3XL-4XL	2-1/2 yards	2-1/2 yards

- 3/4" wide waistband elastic
- Thread to match the fabric
- Basic sewing supplies

Pattern Pieces

(located on the pattern tissue)

- Skirt Front
- Skirt Back

Cutting the Pieces

Refer to the layout guide on the tissue sheets and cut the following pieces:

- One skirt front on the fold
- Two skirt backs

Skirt General Construction

All seams are 5/8" unless otherwise noted. To finish the seams, trim the seams to 1/4" and overcast the edges by machine or serger.

1. With right sides together begin at the top edge and stitch the center back seam of the skirt; stop and backstitch at the dot (**fig. 1**). Clip through the seam allowance to the dot (**fig. 1**). Finish the seam allowance and press to one side.

2. Press each back vent facing to the wrong side along the fold line (**fig. 2**).

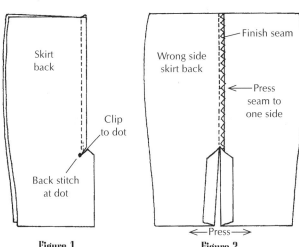

Figure 1

Figure 2

3. Construct a back skirt vent as follows:

Lapped Vent

a. Place the skirt back wrong side up on a flat surface.

b. Open each vent facing and finish the top edge and side edge of the facings by turning under 1/4" and straight stitching in place (**fig. 3**). Press well. Optional: A zigzag or serger may be used to finish the edges (**fig. 4**).

c. Place the skirt right side up on a flat surface.

d. The right vent facing will be extended (**fig. 5**). The left vent facing will be folded in place and overlap the right vent facing. Be sure the hem edges are aligned.

e. Pin across the top edge of the vent. Straight stitch through all layers following the angle of the vent facing as marked on the pattern to secure the top edge of the vent (**fig. 5**).

Open Vent

a. Place the skirt back wrong side up on a flat surface.

b. Open each vent facing and finish the top edge and side edge of the facings by turning under 1/4" and straight stitching in place (**see fig. 3**). Press well. Optional: A zigzag or serger may be used to finish the edges (**see fig. 4**).

c. With the skirt back wrong side up, fold the vent facings in place along the fold lines (**fig. 6**).

d. Hand whip or topstitch along the top edge of the vent following the angle of the vent facing to secure the top edge of the vent (**fig. 6**).

4. Place the skirt back and skirt front right sides together matching the notches; stitch the side seams. Finish the seams and press the seams toward the skirt back (**fig. 7**).

5. Press 1/4" to the wrong side along the top edge of the skirt (**fig. 7**).

6. Fold the casing to the wrong side along the fold line. Press in place (**fig. 7**).

7. Straight stitch very close to the lower edge of the casing, leaving a small opening at the center back seam to insert the elastic. Topstitch very close to the upper edge of the casing; do not leave an opening (**fig. 8**).

8. Hem the skirt with the vent facings open. Turn under 1/4", then 1-1/2". Press in place. Stitch the hem by hand or machine (**fig. 9**).

9. Re-fold the vent facings in place as before.

10. Run the elastic through the casing of the skirt; overlap the ends approximately 1/2" and pin with a safety pin. Try on the skirt and adjust the elastic to a comfortable fit. Cut away excess elastic, leaving a 1/2" overlap. Stitch the overlapped ends of the elastic with a straight stitch or zigzag (**fig. 10**).

11. Stretch the waist of the skirt to make the elastic slip into place in the casing.

12. Straight stitch the opening closed (**fig. 11**).

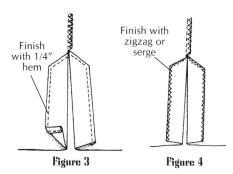

Finish with 1/4" hem

Finish with zigzag or serge

Figure 3   **Figure 4**

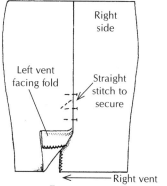

Right side

Left vent facing fold

Straight stitch to secure

Right vent facing extended

Figure 5

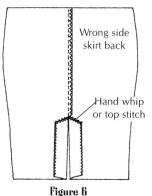

Wrong side skirt back

Hand whip or top stitch

Figure 6

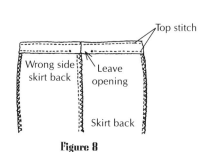

Top stitch

Wrong side skirt back

Leave opening

Skirt back

Figure 8

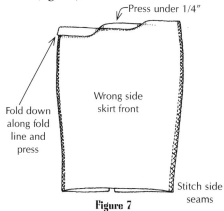

Press under 1/4"

Fold down along fold line and press

Wrong side skirt front

Stitch side seams

Figure 7

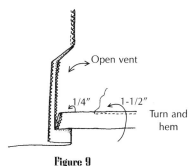

Open vent

1/4"   1-1/2"

Turn and hem

Figure 9

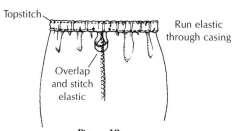

Topstitch

Run elastic through casing

Overlap and stitch elastic

Figure 10

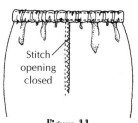

Stitch opening closed

Figure 11

Beaded Embroidered Jacket and Dress

Sometimes you just want a perfect dress and jacket for a special occasion. The wonderful thing about this jacket and dress pattern is that you can make it as dressy or as casual as you wish. It is also the perfect pallet for machine embroidery or hand embroidery. This gorgeous sage green ensemble fits the bill with elegance and style and lots of chances to stitch fabulous stitches with your favorite embroidery machine. The fabric on the sage green jacket is sheer. The embellishment is with silk ribbon bobbin work and double scalloped stitching. The same sheer fabric is used for the overdress over a lining. There is beautiful tone-on-tone double scalloped stitching at the hemline of the dress as well as more silk ribbon bobbin work. Both the dress and the jacket have machine embroideries and scallops. Notice the delicate beadwork on top of the machine embroidery. Made by Diane Witt of Singer, this dress is just perfect for your dress up occasions where you want to look spectacular.

This jacket was made with reference to the Jacket General Directions, Unlined Version found on page 7.
This dress was made with reference to the Dress/Top General Directions found on page 4.

Supplies

- Refer to Jacket General Directions for the fabric yardage requirements and add the requirements for the main fabric and the contrast fabric. The jacket is made entirely from the sheer crepe.
- Refer to the Dress/Top General Directions for the fabric yardage requirements. The fabric for the dress is sheer crepe. The same amount of fabric is required for the lining.
- Thread to match the fabric
- Two spools of decorative rayon thread to match the fabric
- Pearl Crown thread #8 to match the fabric

- 2mm silk ribbon to match the fabric (the dress made as pictured used approximately 75 yards)
- Medium to heavyweight water-soluble stabilizer (WSS)*
- KK2000 (temporary spray adhesive) used to adhere the stabilizer to the fabric
- Small beads to match the fabric
- 1.6/70 twin needle
- Curved-tip embroidery scissors
- Machine embroidery designs**
- Lace shaping board
- Basic sewing supplies

*Bobbin work is used to embellish this garment. Any time bobbin work is used, the chosen fabric must be washable. The stabilizer must be removed by immersing the garment in water.

**NOTE: This jacket was embroidered using a Singer Quantum XL5000. The embroideries for the jacket are built-in designs, Hungarian Lace Pattern. You may use these embroideries or substitute other embroideries that measure approximately 1-1/2" to 1-3/4" wide with a 5" to 6" repeat. To reproduce the jacket and dress as shown, requires a sewing machine with a built-in satin stitch scallop. Or you may use the scallop template given and stitch a scallop using a satin stitch on your machine.

Pattern Pieces

(located on the pattern tissue)

- Jacket Upper Front
- Jacket Lower Front
- Jacket Lower Front Overlay
- Jacket Back
- Jacket Side Back
- Jacket Upper Sleeve
- Jacket Lower Sleeve
- Jacket Shoulder to Tie Neck Ruffle
- Dress/Top Front
- Dress/Top Back

Templates

(found on the tissue pattern)

- Optional: Jacket and Dress Scallop Template
- Serpentine Template

Read all instructions for this garment including the referenced General Directions before cutting or constructing the garment.

Cutting and Preparing the Pieces

Cut the following pieces from the sheer crepe:

- Two Jacket Lower Fronts
- One Jacket Back on the fold
- Two Jacket Side Backs
- Two Jacket Upper Sleeves
- Bias strips 1-3/4" wide to go around the neckline and down the center front of the jacket
- Two bias strips 1-3/4" by 24" for the jacket ties

Trace the following pattern pieces onto blocks of sheer crepe fabric larger than the given pattern pieces:

- Two Jacket Lower Front Overlays, squaring off the front curve of the overlay
- Two Jacket Upper Fronts
- Two Jacket Lower Sleeves
- Two Jacket Shoulder to Tie Neck Ruffles

- Refer to the Dress/Top General Directions, Cutting and Preparing the Pieces and cut the pieces listed for the dress from the sheer crepe. Cut the same pieces from the lining fabric, omitting the bias strips. Be sure to remove the seam allowances from the neckline and armholes.

Jacket Embroidery and Embellishments

1. Place one upper front block onto a lace shaping board with wrong side up. Re-trace the pattern outline onto the wrong side of the fabric block.
2. Mark the 5/8" seam allowance along the lower edge of the jacket upper front.
3. Measure 1-1/2" above the seam line and draw a line. Continue drawing lines 1-1/2" apart until the drawn upper front is filled (**fig. 1**).
4. Repeat steps 1 through 3 for the other upper front block.
5. Repeat the steps above for the two lower front overlay blocks, marking the seam line across the top edge and measuring downward (**fig. 2**).
6. Wind several bobbins with the pearl cotton thread and lay the bobbins aside.
7. Wind several bobbins with the silk ribbon and lay the bobbins aside.
8. Place a pearl cotton bobbin in the machine, bypassing or loosening the bobbin tension, and place sewing thread in the needle.
9. Place WSS under the fabric. With the wrong side up, stitch the chosen embroidery on every other line, beginning with the one closest to the seam allowance line (**fig. 3**).
10. Complete the embroidery on the remaining upper front piece and the two front overlay pieces, beginning with the line closest to the seam allowance (**refer to figure 3**).
11. Place a silk ribbon bobbin in the machine, by-passing or loosening the bobbin tension and place sewing thread in the needle.
12. Trace the serpentine template along the remaining lines (excluding the seam allowance lines) on all pieces.
13. Place WSS under the fabric. From the wrong side of the fabric, straight stitch (L=2.5) along the serpentine line (**fig. 4**).
14. If your machine has a built-in serpentine stitch, you may use this stitch and the appropriate machine foot in place of the template.
15. Repeat steps 13 and 14 for the remaining pieces.

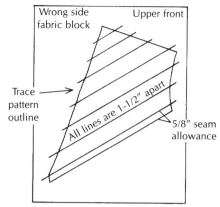

Figure 1

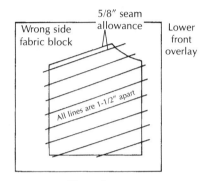

Figure 2

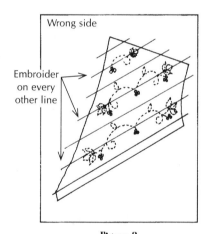

Figure 3

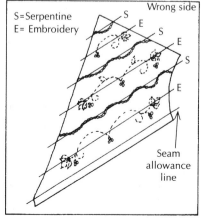

Figure 4

16. Finish the lower edge of the front overlays using one of the methods below:

Built-In Machine Scallop Version

1. Set your machine for the scallop length desired.
2. Place the twin needle in the machine, threaded with the decorative rayon thread in both needles and in the bobbin.
3. On the right side of the overlays, stitch the scallop approximately 5/8" from the lower edge of the overlays (**fig. 5**).
4. Place a silk ribbon bobbin in the machine, by-passing or loosening the tension, and place regular sewing thread in the needle.
5. From the wrong side of the fabric, straight stitch (L=2.5) in the groove of the twin needle satin stitch scallop (**fig. 6**). The silk ribbon portion of the stitch will be on the right side of the fabric.
6. Trim away the excess fabric very close to the scallop using the embroidery scissors (**fig. 6**).

Template Scallop Version

1. Trace the scallop template placing the designated line along the lower edge of the overlay.
2. Place decorative rayon thread in both the needle (single needle) and the bobbin.

3. Stitch a satin stitch along the drawn template line (**fig. 7**). You may gradually decrease the width of the stitch as you approach the point of the scallop and increase to the original width as you exit the scallop. Or, you may wish to stitch the scallop to the point, pivot and continue stitching.
4. Place a silk ribbon bobbin in the machine, by-passing or loosening the tension, and place regular sewing thread in the needle.
5. From the wrong side of the fabric, straight stitch (L=2.5) along the top edge of the satin stitch scallop (**fig. 8**). The silk ribbon portion of the stitch will be on the right side of the fabric.
6. Trim away the excess fabric very close to the scallop using the embroidery scissors (**fig. 8**).

17. Cut out the overlays and upper front pieces along the pattern lines.
18. Hem the inside edge of the overlays by turning under 1/4" then 3/8" and topstitching in place with regular sewing thread (**fig. 9**). Lay the overlays aside.
19. Finish the bottom edge of the lower sleeves using either the Built-In Machine Scallop Version or the Template Scallop Version above (**refer to figures 5 through 8 above**).

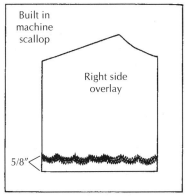

Built in machine scallop

Right side overlay

5/8"

Figure 5

Embroidery NOT shown on remaining upper front and overlay drawings

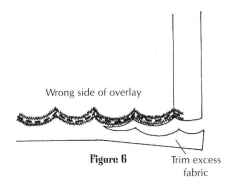

Wrong side of overlay

Figure 6

Trim excess fabric

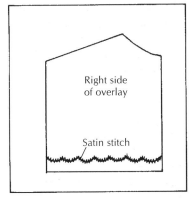

Right side of overlay

Satin stitch

Figure 7

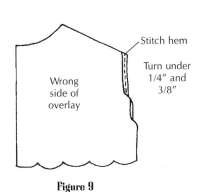

Stitch hem

Turn under 1/4" and 3/8"

Wrong side of overlay

Figure 9

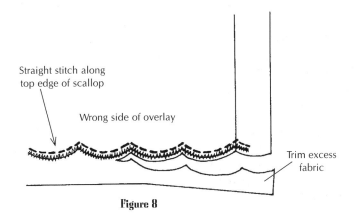

Straight stitch along top edge of scallop

Wrong side of overlay

Trim excess fabric

Figure 8

20. Cut out the lower sleeves along the pattern lines and lay them aside.

21. Using decorative rayon thread in the needle and bobbin, machine satin stitch along the drawn outside edge of the neck ruffle (**fig. 10**).

22. Place a silk ribbon bobbin in the machine, bypassing or loosening the tension, and place regular sewing thread in the needle.

23. From the wrong side of the fabric, straight stitch (L=2.5) along the inside edge of the satin stitch. The silk ribbon portion of the stitch will be on the right side of the fabric (**fig. 11**).

24. Trim away the excess fabric very close to the outside edge of the satin stitch using the embroidery scissors (**fig. 11**).

25. Cut out the neck ruffle along the pattern lines (**fig. 12**). Lay the neck ruffle aside.

Jacket Construction

All seams are 5/8" unless otherwise noted. To finish the seams, trim the seams to 1/4" and overcast the edges by machine or serger.

1. Refer to the Jacket General Directions, General Construction and complete the following:
   a. Steps 2 through 4 for both sides of the jacket front
   b. Steps 6 through 8 for the jacket back
   c. Steps 12 and 13 to construct the sleeves

2. Remove the 5/8" seam allowance from the neck edge and down the front of the jacket (**refer to figure 11 in the Jacket General Directions**).

3. Finish the bottom edge of the jacket using either the Built-In Machine Scallop Version or the Template Scallop Version above. The scallop is stitched approximately 5/8" from the bottom raw edge of the jacket (**refer to figures 5 through 8 above**).

4. Refer to the Jacket General Directions, Unlined Jacket Version and complete steps 3 through 9.

5. Refer to the technique, Creating a Turned Cord (found on page 100) and create two cords for the jacket ties from the bias strips.

6. Attach the ties on the wrong side of the jacket at the center front (**refer to figure 22 in the Jacket General Directions**).

7. Optional: Embellish the embroidery with beads sewn on by hand.

Dress Construction

All seams are 5/8" unless otherwise noted. To finish the seams, trim the seams to 1/4" and overcast the edges by machine or serger.

1. Refer to the Dress/Top General Directions, Construction and complete steps 2 through 4 for the sheer dress and the lining.

2. Stitch and finish the side seams of the sheer dress.

3. Stitch and finish the side seams of the lining.

4. Finish the bottom edge of the <u>sheer dress</u> using either the Built-In Machine Scallop Version or the Template Scallop Version above (**refer to figures 5 through 8 above**). The scallop is stitched approximately 5/8" from the bottom raw edge of the dress.

5. Trim 5/8" from the bottom edge of the dress lining to shorten the lining.

6. Hem the dress lining by turning under 1/4" and then 3/8" and topstitching in place.

7. Place the sheer dress over the lining with the wrong side of the dress to the right side of the lining. Stitch the two together close to the raw edges of the armholes and neckline (**fig. 13**).

8. Refer to the Dress/Top General Directions, Construction and complete steps 1 and steps 5 through 7, treating the dress and lining as one.

9. Stitch the bias to the armholes in the same manner as the neck bias, beginning and ending at the side seam.

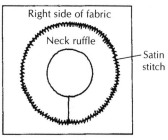

Right side of fabric

Neck ruffle

Satin stitch

Figure 10

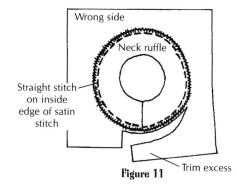

Wrong side

Neck ruffle

Straight stitch on inside edge of satin stitch

Figure 11

Trim excess

Neck ruffle

Figure 12

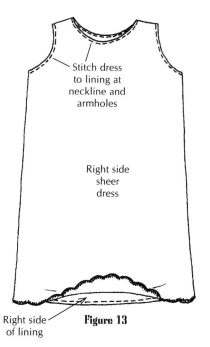

Stitch dress to lining at neckline and armholes

Right side sheer dress

Right side of lining

Figure 13

Beaded Fringe Top

If you want a quick top for someone very stylish in your family, here is your sewing project. Just too cute is this adorable beaded fringe top made of a turquoise gabardine fabric. The neckline and sleeves are finished with a bias binding. The wonderful beading is in shades of brown, black, blue, green, red, white and gold. The top is lined in the same fabric. This top was made by Pam Mahshie of Babylock.

This top was made with reference to the Dress/Top General Directions found on page 4.

Supplies
- Refer to the Dress/Top General Directions for fabric requirements for the Top. Purchase the same amount listed for the top and for the lining.
- Beaded trim
  - XS - LG   1-1/2 yards
  - XL - 4XL   2 yards
- Thread to match the fabric
- Basic sewing supplies

Pattern pieces
(located on the pattern tissue)
- Dress/Top Front
- Dress/Top Back

Read all instructions for this garment including the referenced General Directions before cutting or constructing the garment.

Cutting and Preparing the Pieces
- Refer to the Dress/Top General Directions, Cutting and Preparing the Pieces and follow the steps given for both the main fabric and the lining, cutting along the line designated for the top.

Construction
All seams are 5/8" unless otherwise noted. To finish the seams, trim the seams to 1/4" and overcast the edges by machine or serger.

1. Refer to the Dress/Top General Directions and complete steps 2 through 4 for both the main fabric and the lining.
2. Stitch the side seams of both the main fabric and the lining.

3. Beginning at one side seam, place the beaded trim along the lower edge of the main fabric top, right sides together and stitch in place with a 1/2″ seam allowance. The stitching should be very close to the beads (**fig. 1**).

4. Place the main top and the lining right sides together, one inside the other, sandwiching the beads between the two layers.

5. Restitch on the same stitching line used to join the beads.

6. Turn the top and the lining so they are now wrong sides together with the beads hanging below the hemline.

7. Match the neckline and armholes, basting together close to the edge of the fabric (**fig. 2**).

8. Refer to the Dress/Top General Directions and complete steps 1 and 5 through 8.

9. Finish the bias armholes the same as for the neckline.

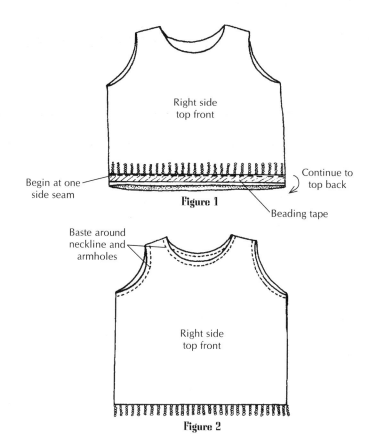

Right side top front

Begin at one side seam

Continue to top back

Beading tape

Figure 1

Baste around neckline and armholes

Right side top front

Figure 2

Women's Size Chart

Size	2-4 XS	6-8 SM	10-12 MD	14-16 LG	18-20 XL	22-24 2XL	26-28 3XL	30-32 4XL
BUST	31	34	37	40	44	48	52	56
WAIST	23	26	29	32	36	40	44	48
HIP	33	36	39	42	46	50	54	58

Bleeding Hearts Jacket and Dress

Silk dupioni is Beverley Sheldrick's favorite fabric and silk ribbon embroidery is her favorite embroidery. For years she has been delighting our Martha's Sewing room audiences with her magic with silk ribbon and a needle. This gorgeous black jacket and matching dress is elegant and will fit almost any occasion. Beverley suggested that this jacket will go with almost anything in almost any color in addition to the matching dress. Silk ribbon embroidered bleeding hearts and side stitched rosebuds are stitched on the front as well as the back of the jacket. The colors used are several shades of pink for the flowers with brown and green for the stems. On the back there is a wonderful periwinkle blue ribbon stitched down with French knots which flows down the back of the jacket. When this jacket is made with a relatively stiff fabric, the front folds over in an asymmetrical way making it very stylish and unusual.

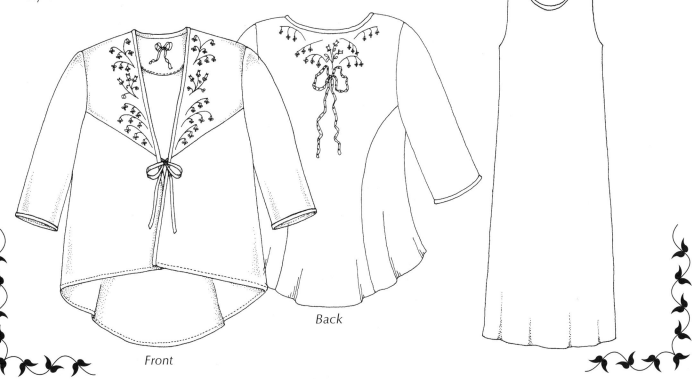

Front

Back

Supplies

- Refer to Jacket General Directions for the fabric yardage requirements. Purchase the same amount of lining as fabric for the jacket.
- Refer to the Dress/Top General Directions for the fabric yardage requirements.
- YLI silk ribbon in the following colors and sizes:

7mm	Pink	#5
7mm	Green	#18
4mm	Green	#18
4mm	Purple	#101
4mm	Medium Pink	#111
4mm	Rose	#152

- DMC floss in the following colors:

Med. Tan	#435
Lt. Green	#3348
Purple	#210

- #24 or #26 tapestry needles
- Thread to match the fabric
- Basic sewing supplies

Pattern Pieces

(located on the pattern tissue)

- Jacket Upper Front
- Jacket Lower Front
- Jacket Back
- Jacket Side Back
- Jacket Upper Sleeve (alter pattern as shown in **figure 1** to remove V-shape from sleeve)
- Dress/Top Front
- Dress/Top Back

Templates

(located on the tissue pattern)

- Back Lining Neckline Inset and Embroidery
- Jacket Upper Front Embroidery
- Jacket Back Embroidery

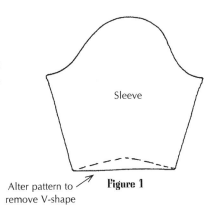

Sleeve

Alter pattern to remove V-shape

Figure 1

Read all instructions for this garment including the referenced General Directions before cutting or constructing the garment.

Cutting and Preparing the Pieces

(refer to the layouts on the pattern tissue sheets)

Trace the following pieces onto a silk dupioni rectangle slightly larger than the pattern piece:

- Two Jacket Upper Fronts
- One Jacket Back on the fold
- One Back Lining Neckline Inset

Cut out the following pieces from the silk dupioni fabric:

- Two Jacket Lower Fronts
- Two Jacket Side Backs
- Two Jacket Upper Sleeves
- Bias strips 1-3/4" wide to go around the neckline, down the center front of the jacket and at the edge of each sleeve (Stitch the bias strips together to make one continuous length of bias. Fold the bias in half lengthwise, matching the raw edges; press a crease, being careful not to stretch the bias. Refer to figures 13 and 14 in the Jacket General Directions.)
- Two bias strips 1-3/4" by 24" for constructing the turned cords

Cut the following pieces from the lining fabric:

- Two Jacket Upper Fronts
- One Jacket Back on the fold
- Two Jacket Lower Fronts
- Two Jacket Side Backs
- Two Jacket Upper Sleeves

Cut the following pieces from the dress fabric:

- One dress/top front on the fold
- One dress/top back on the fold

Jacket

Completing the Silk Ribbon Embroidery

1. Trace the embroidery templates onto the jacket back, jacket upper front and back lining neckline inset rectangles. Refer to the finished drawing for aid in placement. Refer to the Embroidery Techniques and the embroidery templates to complete the embroideries.
2. When the embroidery is complete, cut out the pieces.

Jacket Construction

All seams are 5/8" unless otherwise noted. To finish the seams, trim the seams to 1/4" and overcast the edges by machine or serger.

1. Stitch a line of lengthened straight stitching for easing across the upper edge of the jacket lower front (**fig. 2**).
2. Place the jacket upper front to the jacket lower front with right sides together; stitch the seam, easing the edge of the jacket lower front to fit the jacket upper front (**fig. 3**).
3. Repeat steps 1 and 2 for the other side of the jacket front. Press the seams toward the upper front.
4. Refer to the Jacket General Directions, General Construction and complete steps 6 through 8.
5. Fold the sleeve with right sides together; stitch and finish the seam. Press the seam toward the front.
6. Stitch a row of lengthened machine stitching between the notches on the sleeve cap for easing (**fig. 4**). Pin the sleeves into the armholes, matching the side seams of the jacket to the sleeve seams. Stitch and finish the seams. Press the seams toward the sleeves (**fig. 5**).
7. Finish the lower raw edge of the jacket hemline with a zigzag or serge. Fold 5/8" to the inside to form the jacket hem and press (**fig. 6**). Hem the jacket by machine or hand.

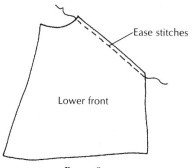

Figure 2

> **NOTE**
> Drawings do not show embroidery detail

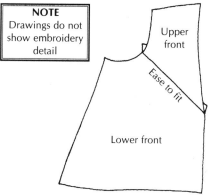

Figure 3

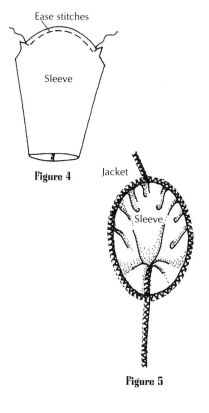

Figure 4

Figure 5

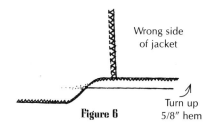

Figure 6

8. Complete steps 1 through 6 above to construct the lining. Attach the neckline inset as follows:

   a. Straight stitch around the curve of the inset along the drawn stitching lines (**fig. 7**). Cut out the inset 1/4″ from the stitching along the cutting lines (**fig. 8**).

   b. Finger press the raw edge of the inset under along the stitching line, clipping through the seam allowance along the curves if necessary (**fig. 9**)

   c. Position the inset onto the right side of the lining at the center back neckline.

   d. Topstitch the inset to the lining very close to the folded edge (**fig. 10**).

   e. Baste the inset to the lining along the neckline (**fig. 10**).

9. Finish the lower edge of the jacket lining with a zigzag or serge. Turn up a 3/4″ hem along the bottom edge of the jacket lining and press. Hem the jacket lining by machine or hand.

10. Slip the jacket lining into the jacket with the wrong side of the lining to the wrong side of the jacket, matching the seams and aligning the bottom edges of the sleeves and front of the jacket. Baste the layers together along the jacket fronts, neckline and bottom edges of sleeves (**fig. 11**).

11. Pin the bias tape to the right side of the sleeve, beginning at the sleeve seam with the end folded back; match the raw edges of the bias tape to the raw edge of the sleeve (**fig. 12**). When the bias has been pinned around the sleeve, allow the end of the bias to overlap the beginning by approximately 1/2″. Trim away the excess bias. Stitch the bias to the sleeve with a 1/4″ seam (**fig. 13**). Repeat for the other sleeve.

12. Refer to the Jacket General Directions, Unlined Jacket Version and complete step 8 to finish the bias at the edge of each sleeve.

13. Refer to the Jacket General Directions, Unlined Jacket Version and complete steps 6 through 8, treating the jacket and the lining as one layer.

14. Slipstitch the jacket lining to the jacket at the hemline.

15. Refer to the technique, Creating a Turned Cord found on page 100 and construct two turned cords for the jacket ties.

16. Attach the cords to the jacket front by hand or machine (refer to figure 22 in the General Jacket Directions).

Dress Construction

All seams are 5/8″ unless otherwise noted. To finish the seams, trim the seams to 1/4″ and overcast the edges by machine or serger.

Refer to Dress/Top General Directions and complete all steps.

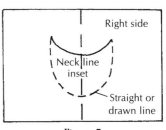

Figure 7

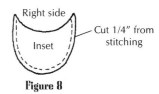

Figure 8

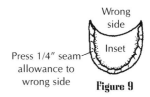

Figure 9

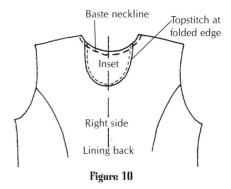

Figure 10

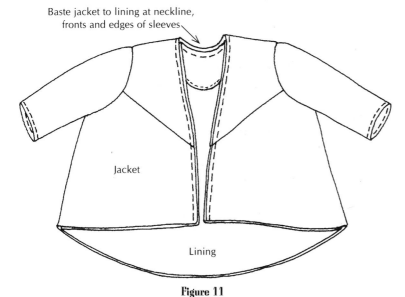

Baste jacket to lining at neckline, fronts and edges of sleeves

Jacket

Lining

Figure 11

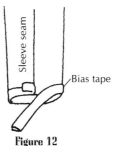

Figure 12

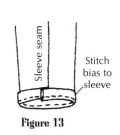

Figure 13

Burn-Out Over Blouse, Top and Skirt

Created by Sue Pennington Stewart, this blue outfit consists of the Over Blouse, top and skirt. The fabric is a silk/rayon burn-out velvet with stretch velvet binding at the neckline. The top and skirt are made of a stretch velvet type fabric. A turned cord of the stretch velvet is run through the casing in the back of the Over Blouse to pull in the fullness. The back of the skirt has a lapped vent opening.

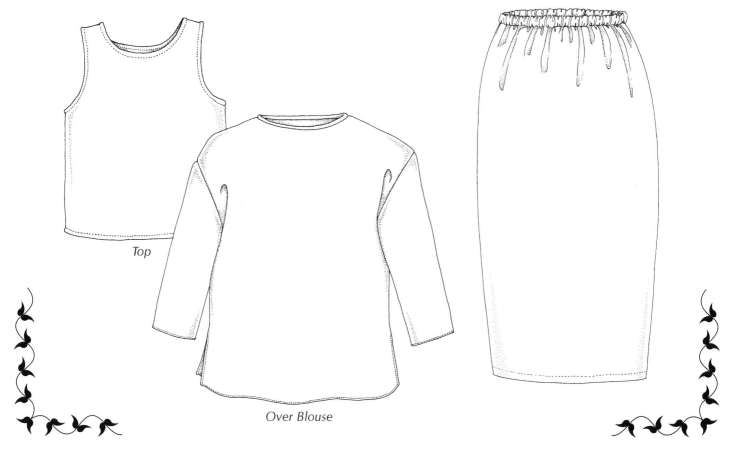

Top

Over Blouse

This Over Blouse was made with reference to the Over Blouse General Directions found on page 11.
This top was made with reference to the Dress/Top General Directions found on page 4.
This skirt was made with reference to the Skirt General Directions with the Lapped Vent found on page 15.

Supplies
- Refer to the Over Blouse General Directions for fabric requirements
- Refer to the Dress/Top General Directions for fabric requirements for the top
- Refer to the Skirt General Directions for fabric requirements adding 1/2 yard to the requirements to make the Over Blouse turned cord and the bias neckline
- Thread to match the fabric
- Velvet board for pressing
- Basic sewing supplies

Pattern Pieces
(found on the pattern tissue)
- Over Blouse Front
- Over Blouse Back
- Over Blouse Sleeve
- Over Blouse Back Tie Casing
- Over Blouse Back Tie
- Refer to the Dress/Top General Directions for pattern pieces
- Refer to Skirt General Directions for pattern pieces

Read all instructions for this garment including the referenced General Directions before cutting or constructing the garment.

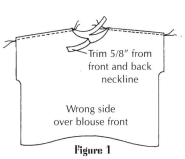

Trim 5/8" from front and back neckline

Wrong side over blouse front

Figure 1

Cutting and Preparing the Pieces

- Refer to the over blouse layout guide (found on the pattern tissue) and cut the following pieces from the burn-out fabric:
  - One over blouse front on the fold - mark the armhole notches and side notch
  - One over blouse back on the fold - mark the casing placement, armhole notches and side notch
  - Two over blouse sleeves - mark the notches and the shoulder dot
  - One over blouse back tie casing
- Cut the following from interfacing:
  - One Over Blouse Front Facing on the fold
  - One Over Blouse Back Facing on the fold

- Refer to the dress/top layout guide (found on the pattern tissue) and cut the following pieces from the stretch velvet:
  - 1" wide strips cut across the width of the fabric- enough to go around the neckline of over blouse. Piece together if necessary.
  - Two over blouse back ties
  - Refer to the Dress/Top General Directions, Cutting and Preparing the Pieces for cutting directions
  - Refer to the Skirt General Directions, Cutting and Preparing the Pieces for cutting directions

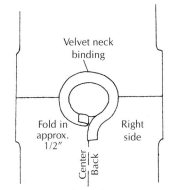

Velvet neck binding

Fold in approx. 1/2"

Right side

Center Back

Figure 2

Over Blouse Construction

All seams are 5/8" unless otherwise noted. To finish the seams, trim the seams to 1/4" and overcast the edges by machine or serger. French seams may be used. Refer to French Seam (found on page 104).

1. Place the over blouse front and the over blouse back with right sides together, matching the shoulder seams. Stitch the shoulder seams (**fig. 1**). Finish the seams, and press the seams toward the over blouse back.
2. Trim 5/8" from the front and back neck edge of the over blouse (**fig. 1**).
3. Beginning at the center back neck edge, place the velvet strip right sides together along the neckline matching the raw edge of the strip to the raw edge of the neckline. Fold the end of the strip in approximately 1/2" (**fig. 2**). When the strip has been pinned around the neck edge, allow the end to overlap the beginning by approximately 1/2" (**refer to fig. 3**). Trim away the excess strip.
4. Hand baste the strip to the neckline of the over blouse to prevent stretching. Stitch the strip to the over blouse with a 1/4" seam (**fig. 3**).

5. Wrap the strip over the seam allowance and turn under the inside long edge of the strip. The folded edge of the strip will be even with the stitching line. Pin in place on the inside of the over blouse (**fig. 4**).
6. Hand whip the folded edge of the strip in place at the seam line (**fig. 5**).
7. Stitch a row of lengthened machine stitching between the notches on the sleeve for easing (**fig. 6**).
8. Match the notches on the top edge of the sleeve to the notches on the over blouse. Also, match the dot on the sleeve to the shoulder seam. Stitch the sleeve to the over blouse (**fig. 7**). Press the seam allowance toward the over blouse.

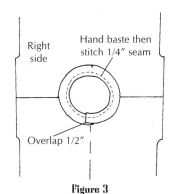

Right side

Hand baste then stitch 1/4" seam

Overlap 1/2"

Figure 3

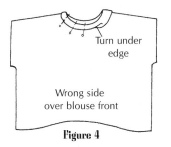

Turn under edge

Wrong side over blouse front

Figure 4

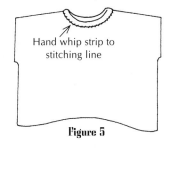

Hand whip strip to stitching line

Figure 5

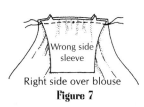

Wrong side sleeve

Right side over blouse

Figure 7

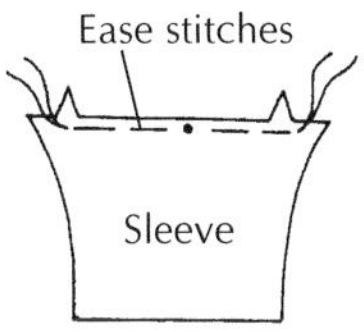

Ease stitches

Sleeve

Figure 6

9. Hem the lower edge of each sleeve as follows:
   a. Machine straight stitch 3/8" from the raw edge (**fig. 8**).
   b. Press the raw edge toward the wrong side exactly on the stitching line (**fig 9**).
   c. Machine stitch very close to the fold (**fig. 10**).
   d. Trim close to the stitching.
   e. Fold the hem up 1/4" and stitch again (**fig. 11**).

10. Place the back tie casing pattern onto the over blouse back and mark the two buttonholes in the center of the over blouse back (**fig. 12**).

11. Place stabilizer or interfacing on the wrong side of the over blouse back under the buttonhole marks. Stitch two 1/2" buttonholes at the placement markings in the center of the over blouse back. Cut the buttonholes open.

12. Refer to the Over Blouse General Directions, Construction, and complete steps 8 through 12, placing the casing on the **wrong** side of the over blouse back.

13. With right sides together, match the front to the back at the edge of the sleeve, the underarm seam and the bottom edge of the over blouse. Stitch and finish the sleeve and side seams of the over blouse, beginning at the bottom of the sleeve and stopping at the notch just below the back casing (**refer to fig. 13**). Backstitch at the notch to secure. This will create a vent on each side of the over blouse.

14. Clip through the seam allowance on each side of the over blouse at the point where the stitching stops (**fig. 13**).

15. Hem the bottom edge of the over blouse front and back and the vent openings by turning under approximately 1/4" and 1/4" again and straight stitching in place (**fig. 14**).

16. Pull up the back ties and tie into a bow at the center of the over blouse back.

Skirt Construction

All seams are 5/8" unless otherwise noted. To finish the seams, trim the seams to 1/4" and overcast the edges by machine or serger.

Refer to the Skirt General Directions and complete all steps with the lapped vent version.

Top Construction

All seams are 5/8" unless otherwise noted. To finish the seams, trim the seams to 1/4" and overcast the edges by machine or serger.

Refer to Dress/Top General Directions and complete all steps.

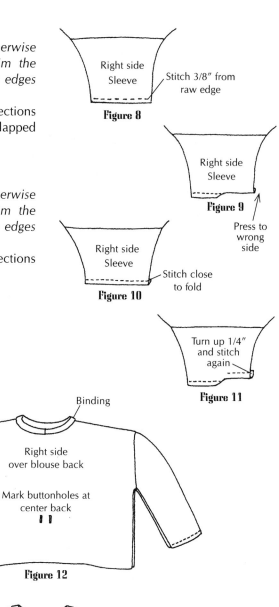

Right side Sleeve — Stitch 3/8" from raw edge

Figure 8

Right side Sleeve — Press to wrong side

Figure 9

Right side Sleeve — Stitch close to fold

Figure 10

Turn up 1/4" and stitch again

Figure 11

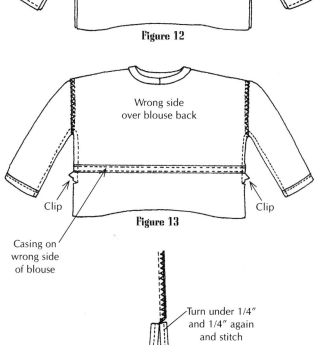

Binding

Right side over blouse back

Mark buttonholes at center back

Figure 12

Wrong side over blouse back

Clip   Clip

Casing on wrong side of blouse

Figure 13

Turn under 1/4" and 1/4" again and stitch

Figure 14

Canterbury Bells
Over Blouse and Skirt

This white linen over blouse and skirt set is appropriate for almost every occasion where one wants to look gorgeous and elegant. White handkerchief linen is used for both pieces. The pockets have a turned cord tie to hold in the fullness. Three rows of blue machine topstitching embellish the neckline. The thread for this topstitching is 30 weight which really shows up on the stark white handkerchief linen. Just under the center front of the V'd neckline are Canterbury bells done in blue silk ribbon. The centers of the flowers have yellow silk ribbon and embroidery floss. The stems are a pale green and the silk ribbon stitches form the leaves. More silk ribbon embroidery is found at the bottom of each sleeve. A turned cord tie through the back casing holds in the fullness at the over blouse back waistline. The skirt has an elastic waistline and an open vent in the back. This gorgeous outfit was made by Beverley Sheldrick of New Zealand.

This over blouse was made with reference to the Over Blouse General Directions found on page 11.
This skirt was made with reference to the Skirt General Directions with the Open Vent found on page 15.

Supplies

- Refer to Over Blouse General Directions for fabric requirements
- Refer to Skirt General Directions for fabric requirements
- Lightweight thread to match the fabric
- Lightweight thread to match the blue silk ribbon
- 30 weight thread for topstitching to match the blue silk ribbon
- Silk ribbon in the following sizes and colors:

7mm	Blue	#44
7mm	Green	#33
4mm	Green	#32
4mm	Gold	#147

- Green DMC floss (#503)
- #8 crewel or #8 sharp hand sewing needle
- #24 or #26 tapestry needles
- Small embroidery hoop
- Basic sewing supplies

Pattern Pieces
(located on the pattern tissue)
- Over Blouse Front with the V neckline option (curved hem option)
- Over Blouse Front Facing
- Over Blouse Back (curved hem option)
- Over Blouse Back Facing
- Over Blouse Sleeve

- Over Blouse Sleeve Wrist Binding
- Over Blouse Pocket
- Over Blouse Back Tie Casing
- Over Blouse Back Tie
- Over Blouse Pocket Tie
- Skirt Front
- Skirt Back

Template
(located on the tissue pattern)
- Silk ribbon embroidery templates

Read all instructions for this garment including the referenced General Directions before cutting or constructing the garment.

Cutting the Pieces

- Refer to the Over Blouse General Directions, Cutting the Pieces for cutting directions, cutting the over blouse with the V neckline option.
- After cutting out the pieces, trace the silk ribbon embroidery design from the embroidery template onto the sleeves and neckline. Silk ribbon embroidery should be completed on the sleeves before construction, and on the neckline after construction and topstitching are completed.
- Cut the following from interfacing:
  - One Over Blouse Front Facing on the fold
  - One Over Blouse Back Facing on the fold
- Refer to the Skirt General Directions, Cutting the Pieces for cutting directions.

Over Blouse Construction

All seams are 5/8" unless otherwise noted. To finish the seams, trim the seams to 1/4" and overcast the edges by machine or serger.

NOTE: All stitching noted in the General Directions is completed with lightweight sewing thread to match the linen.

1. Refer to the Over Blouse General Directions and complete steps 1 through 6.
2. Complete the embroidery on the sleeves, referring to the silk ribbon embroidery template and the embroidery techniques (found on pages 106-110).
3. Refer to the Over Blouse General Directions and complete the remaining steps.
4. Pin the neck facing in place. Using the 30 wt. thread and a stitch length of 4.0, stitch three rows of topstitching around the neck edge 3/8" apart; the first row is 3/8" below the neck edge (refer to the finished drawing).

5. Complete the embroidery at the neckline, referring to the silk ribbon embroidery template and the embroidery techniques (found on pages 106-110).

Skirt Construction

All seams are 5/8" unless otherwise noted. To finish the seams, trim the seams to 1/4" and overcast the edges by machine or serger.

1. Refer to the Skirt General Directions and complete all steps with the open vent version. All stitching in the General Directions is completed with lightweight sewing thread to match the linen.
2. Using the 30 weight thread and a stitch length of 4.0, stitch three rows of topstitching around the hemline of the skirt and around the vent opening 3/8" apart; the first row is 3/8" above the skirt bottom edge (refer to the finished drawing of the skirt).

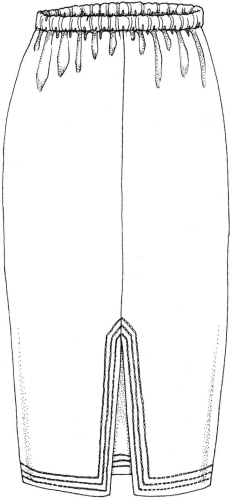

Color Change With
Cover Stitch Top and Skirt

We had the best time trying to photograph this gorgeous and very youthful outfit for the book. Since you have to go outside to make the solar active thread change colors, our model would dash outside and the flowers would turn pink. Then she would dash inside and the colors would fade before our photographer could get the shot. The skirt and short top are made of white handkerchief linen. There are two rows of serger cover stitches on the top and the skirt. Machine embroidered flowers are in-between the two rows of serger stitching. Corded scallops using rayon thread to match the fabric, border the hemline of the top and skirt. The neckline and sleeves have a bias binding of white linen. The skirt has elastic at the waistline. This adorable duo was made by Pam Mahshie of Babylock.

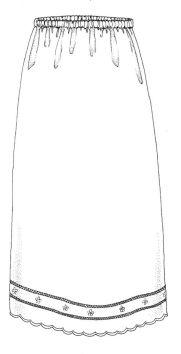

This blouse was made with reference to the Dress/Top General Directions found on page 4.
This skirt was made with reference to the Skirt General Directions with the Lapped Vent found on page 15.

Supplies
- Refer to the Dress/Top General Directions, fabric requirements for the top
- Refer to the Skirt General Directions for fabric requirements for the skirt
- Stabilizer
- Optional: KK2000 (temporary spray adhesive)
- Thread to match the fabric
- 40 wt. decorative rayon thread to match the fabric
- Optional: Solar Active™ Thread* (yellow centers were used for the flowers and pink was used for the cover stitch)
- Gimp cord for satin stitching scallops
- Machine embroidery designs**
- Basic sewing supplies

*Caution: Hot iron may melt thread.
**NOTE: This blouse was embroidered using a Babylock Ellageo. The embroidery for the blouse and skirt is a built-in embroidery on the Ellageo 2 and 3. You may use this embroidery or substitute another embroidery which measure approximately 1" by 1".

Pattern Pieces
(located on the pattern tissue)
- Dress/Top Front
- Dress/Top Back
- Skirt Front
- Skirt Back

Template
(located on the tissue pattern)
- Scallop Template for Top and Skirt

Read all instructions for this garment including the referenced General Directions before cutting or constructing the garment.

Cutting and Preparing the Pieces
- Refer to the layout guide (found on the tissue sheet) and cut the following pieces along the designated cutting line for the top:
  - one top front on the fold Mark the center front
  - one top back on the fold. Mark the center back
- Refer to the layout guide (found on the tissue sheet) and cut the following pieces for the skirt:
  - one skirt front on the fold
  - two skirt backs

Top Construction

All seams are 5/8" unless otherwise noted. To finish the seams, trim the seams to 1/4" and overcast the edges by machine or serger.

1. Refer to the Dress/Top General Directions and complete steps 1 through 9.
2. Place the designated line on the template even with the unfinished edge along the bottom edge of the top.
3. Trace the scallop onto the lower edge of the top. You may need to make one or two scallops more narrow or wider to have them to come out even around the hemline of the top. NOTE: A built-in machine scallop may be used.
4. Place stabilizer beneath the drawn scallops on the bottom edge of the top. Begin at a side seam.
5. Stitch a satin stitch scallop, using rayon thread to match the fabric, around the hemline along the drawn lines. You may gradually decrease the width of the stitch as you approach the point of the scallop and increase to the original width as you exit the scallop. Or, you may wish to stitch the scallop to the point, pivot and continue stitching. Remove the stabilizer and press well.
6. Trim the fabric very close to the satin stitching, being very careful not to cut the stitching (**fig. 1**).
7. Place another strip of stabilizer behind the scallops. KK 2000 may be used to adhere the fabric to the stabilizer.
8. Beginning at a side seam, place the gimp cord against the lower edge of the scallop. Choose a satin stitch width to catch the lower edge of the satin stitch scallops and cover the gimp cord. Stitch over the cord around the scallops using rayon thread to match the fabric (**fig. 2**). When you reach the beginning, cut the cords to meet and continue stitching until the cords are covered.

9. Referring to the template, draw two lines above the scallop for the serger cover stitch (**fig. 3**). Refer to your serger manual for cover stitch instructions. A decorative embroidery stitch or build-in embroidery stitch may be substituted for the cover stitch.
10. Stitch a serger cover stitch using color change thread along the two drawn lines on the right side of the top (**fig. 3**).
11. Beginning at one side seam, measure around the top front and back between the cover stitch lines. Divide this measurement by 8. This will be the distance between the center of the stitched flowers. Adjust the distance between the flowers as desired.
12. Mark the center front between the cover stitch lines. This will be the placement for one flower. Measure over the distance determined in step 11. Mark for another flower. Continue this around the top.
13. Stabilize, hoop and embroider the designs around the top (**refer to the finished drawing**). Remove the stabilizer and press well.

Skirt Construction

All seams are 5/8" unless otherwise noted. To finish the seams, trim the seams to 1/4" and overcast the edges by machine or serger.

1. Refer to the Skirt General Directions and complete steps 1 through 7 and steps 10 through 12, choosing the Lapped Vent Version.
2. Trim 1" from bottom edge of skirt front and back.
3. Refer to the Top Construction above, steps 2 through 13 and complete the scallops, cover stitch and embroidered flowers on the skirt. The same distance may be used between the flowers on the skirt as was used for the top, or the flowers may be spaced further apart. Pin the lap closed before measuring around the skirt. If an embroidered flower falls on the lapped portion of the skirt, open the lap before stitching the flower.

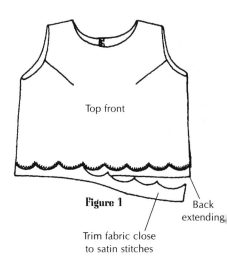

Figure 1

Top front

Back extending

Trim fabric close to satin stitches

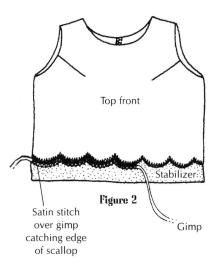

Figure 2

Top front

Stabilizer

Satin stitch over gimp catching edge of scallop

Gimp

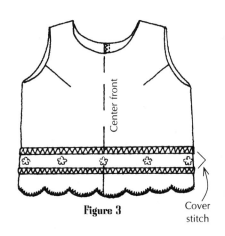

Figure 3

Center front

Cover stitch

Cornelli Lace Jacket and Dress

For the truly special occasion in your life, this just might be the dress and jacket you need. Made by Connie Palmer from Husqvarna/Viking using white handkerchief linen, silk organza and Swiss cotton netting, this is a joy to embroider and stitch if you love sewing machine magic. The ruffled collar is made of three rows of white French insertion with a slightly gathered French edging on the outside. The Cornelli lace overlays are made by either free motion stipple stitching on the netting or by using a built-in stipple stitching on the machine. The trim around each overlay has two rows of white French insertion and one row of flat French edging. All of the rows of French lace are joined with the featherstitch, by machine of course. The upper jacket pieces are made of white linen with strips of white French insertion pinstitched to the linen. The sleeves have one row of white French insertion at the bottom with a beautiful white silk organza "ruffle" made of white French insertion with white French edging on the bottom. Little vents are on the sides of the organza/lace ruffle with tied white bows of silk ribbon at the top. The beautiful one-piece dress makes the perfect backdrop for this stunning white jacket.

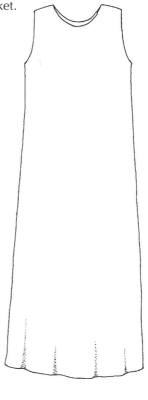

This jacket was made with reference to the General Jacket Directions, Unlined Version found on page 7.
This dress was made with reference to the Dress/Top General Directions found on page 4.

Supplies

- Refer to Jacket General Directions. Main Fabric requirements for linen requirements for the jacket.
- Refer to Dress/Top General Directions for linen fabric requirements for the dress.
- Cotton netting
    - XS - L   5/8 yard
    - XL - 4XL   1 yard
- 1/4 yard silk organza
- 5/8" wide lace insertion (lace A)
    - XS - L   16-1/2 yards
    - XL - 4XL   17-5/8 yards
- 6 yards edging lace (lace B)
- 2-1/8 yards of 1-1/2" wide edging lace (lace C)
- 1-1/3 yards of 1" wide silk satin ribbon for jacket ties

- 50 wt. thread to match 12 wt. thread
- 1-1/3 yards of 1/2" wide silk satin ribbon for jacket sleeves
- #80, #90 and #110 needles
- 12 wt. Sulky thread for stipple stitching
- Washout marker
- 80 wt. thread for lace shaping
- 50 wt. thread for construction
- Heavyweight water-soluble stabilizer
- Lace shaping board
- Basic sewing supplies
- Optional: Hoop (free-motion stipple stitching)

Pattern Pieces
(located on the pattern tissue)

- Jacket Upper Front
- Jacket Lower Front
- Jacket Lower Front Overlay
- Jacket Back
- Jacket Side Back
- Jacket Upper Sleeve
- Jacket Lower Sleeve
- Jacket Shoulder to Tie Neck Ruffle
- Dress/Top Front
- Dress/Top Back

Template
(located on the tissue pattern)

- Curve for Ruffle Front

Read all instructions for this garment including the referenced General Directions before cutting or constructing the garment.

Cutting and Preparing the Pieces

- Cut the following pieces for the jacket from the linen fabric:
  - Two jacket lower fronts
  - One jacket back on the fold
  - Two jacket side backs
  - Two jacket upper sleeves
  - Two rectangles slightly larger than the jacket upper front
- Cut the following pieces for the dress from the linen fabric:
  - One dress front on the fold
  - One dress back on the fold
- Cut the following pieces from the silk organza:
  - Two 9″ by 9″ squares for the ruffles
  - Two rectangles larger than the lower sleeve pattern piece
- Cut a jacket upper front tissue pattern in the chosen size
- Cut a lower sleeve tissue pattern in the chosen size

Refer to Basic Heirloom Techniques (found on page 98) for shaping and attaching lace to fabric.

All seams are 5/8″ unless otherwise noted. To finish the seams, trim the seams to 1/4″ and overcast the edges by machine or serger.

Jacket

Creating the Jacket Upper Front

1. Locate the jacket upper front tissue pattern.
2. Draw a vertical line down the center of the tissue pattern. Draw vertical lines spaced 1-3/8″ apart on each side of the center line (**fig. 1**).
3. Trace this pattern with template lines onto the two rectangles of linen cut for the upper jacket front. Be sure that you have a right and left upper jacket front.
4. Center a strip of lace insertion A over each drawn line (**fig. 2**). Pin in place.
5. Zigzag along the lace headings (**fig. 3**).
6. Slit the fabric behind the lace and press away from the lace (**fig. 4**).
7. Zigzag along the lace headings again from the right side (**fig. 5**).
8. From the wrong side, trim the fabric close to the zigzag (**fig. 6**).
9. Starch and press the piece well.
10. Optional: Pinstitch on each side of the lace strips (**fig. 7**). The straight side of the stitch should be on the fabric, and the "fingers" will stitch into the lace.
11. Repeat steps 4 through 10 for the other jacket upper front.
12. Cut out the jacket upper front pieces along the cutting lines.
13. Lay the jacket upper front pieces aside.

Embellishing the Jacket Back

1. Place the jacket side backs to the jacket back, right sides together and stitch. Trim the seams to 1/8″.
2. Center and shape a strip of lace insertion A over each seam (**fig. 8**).
3. Zigzag both sides of the insertion along the headings (**refer to fig. 3**).
4. On the wrong side, cut the fabric behind the insertion up the center along the seam line (**refer to fig. 4**).
5. Press both sides away from the insertion (**refer to fig. 4**).
6. Zigzag along both lace headings again from the right side (**refer to fig. 5**).
7. On wrong side, trim the fabric very close to the zigzag (**refer to fig. 6**).
8. Pinstitch both sides of the insertion (**refer to fig. 7**).
9. Lay the jacket back aside.

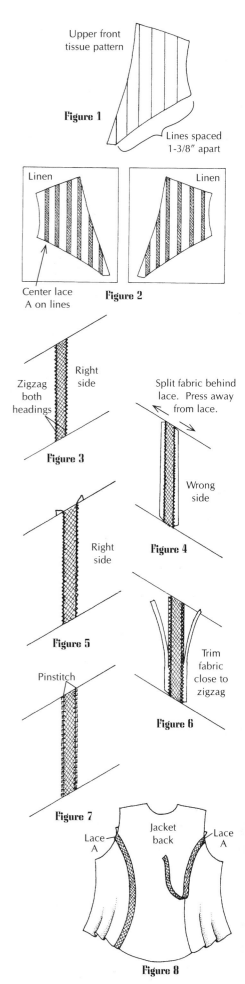

Upper front tissue pattern

Figure 1

Lines spaced 1-3/8″ apart

Linen — Linen

Center lace A on lines

Figure 2

Zigzag both headings — Right side

Figure 3

Split fabric behind lace. Press away from lace.

Wrong side

Figure 4

Right side

Figure 5

Pinstitch

Figure 7

Trim fabric close to zigzag

Figure 6

Lace A — Jacket back — Lace A

Figure 8

Creating the Ruffle

1. Locate the two 9" by 9" squares of silk organza for the ruffle.
2. Trace the inner cutting line and seam line (5/8" inside the cutting line) on the squares (**fig. 9**).
3. Place one of the silk squares on a lace shaping board.
4. Shape a piece of lace A around the circle with the inside edge of the insertion on the seam line (**fig. 9**). Refer to Basic Heirloom Techniques (found on page 98).
5. Zigzag (L=1.5, W=1.5) the inside header (**fig. 9**).
6. Trim the silk 5/8" from the zigzagged lace heading, being very careful not to cut the lace (**fig. 9**).
7. Clip and press the silk seam allowance towards the center of the circle (**fig. 10**) Press well.
8. Zigzag (L=1.5, W=1.5) the header again (**fig. 10**).
9. Trace the neck ruffle onto a square of heavyweight WSS (**fig. 11**).
10 Place a second square of heavy-weight WSS underneath the first.
11. Thread the sewing machine with 12 wt. Sulky thread in the top and bobbin.
12. Place a #90 needle in the machine.
13. Place the lace insertion piece with silk organza attached onto the WSS, matching the cutting and seam lines (**fig. 11**).
14. Shape two additional strips of lace insertion A around the curve of the ruffle, spacing them approximately 1/4" apart (**fig. 11**).
15. Join the laces with a featherstitch (L=3.0, W=6.0) (**fig. 11**). Adjust the stitch as necessary so that the headings of the lace are caught in the stitching.
16. Trace the curve on the ruffle front. Stay-stitch 1/4" inside the curved edges (**fig. 11**).
17. Trim along the curve line 1/4" from the stay stitching (**fig. 11**).
18. Fold under along the stay stitching line and zigzag the folded edge.
19. Measure around the outside edge of the ruffle and cut a piece of lace edging B twice this measurement.

20. Gather the lace to fit the circle.
21. Place two layers of WSS under the curve and attach the edging lace in the same manner as before (**fig. 12**).
22. Soak the ruffle in water until all traces of stabilizer are gone.
23. Air dry and press the ruffle.
24. Cut the inside circle away leaving a 5/8" seam allowance (**fig. 13**).
25. Repeat steps 3 through 24 for the second ruffle.
26. Lay the created ruffles aside.

Creating the Overlay

1. Wash the netting and allow to air dry to pre-shrink. Starch and press the netting.
2. Trace the overlay onto the netting. Cut a square larger than the drawn overlay.
3. Draw a line at an angle from corner to corner (**fig. 14**).
4. Wind five bobbins with #12 wt. Sulky thread.
5. Place one bobbin in the machine, by-passing the tension.
6. Thread the machine with the 50 wt. sewing thread to match.
7. Bring the bobbin thread to the top.
8. Place the netting square right side down on your sewing machine. Place a layer of heavyweight WSS under the netting (**fig. 14**).
9. Select a stipple stitch on your machine and stipple along the drawn line. The side with the bobbin thread is the right side of the stippling (**fig. 14**).
10. Continue adding rows of stippling, lining up the edge of the foot with the previous row and allowing stippling to go slightly beyond drawn lines.
11. If a stipple stitch is not available as an automatic stitch on your machine, the stipple stitch may be done "free-handed". Hoop the netting right side down sandwiched between two layers of WSS and refer to the technique, Stipple Stitching (found on page 104). Complete the stipple stitching on the netting.

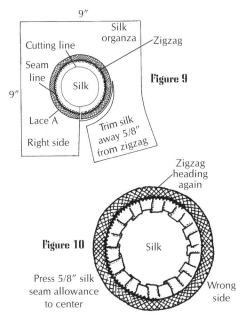

Figure 9

Figure 10

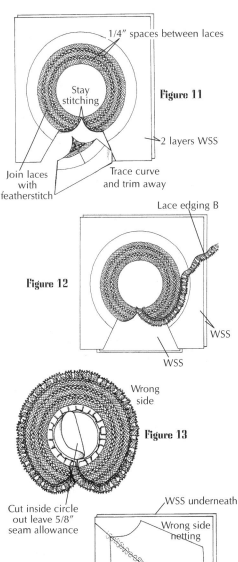

Figure 11

Figure 12

Figure 13

Figure 14

12. Shape a piece of lace insertion A around the curved outer edge of the overlay. Place the outside edge of the insertion even with the drawn cutting line (**fig. 15**). Refer to Basic Heirloom Techniques (found on page 98).

13. Zigzag along the inside lace heading. Trim the netting just beyond the outer lace heading (**fig. 15**).

14. Press the fabric behind the insertion towards the overlay (**fig. 16**).

15. Zigzag along the heading again from the right side.

16. On the wrong side, trim the netting close to the zigzag (**fig. 16**).

17. Place two layers of WSS under the insertion.

18. Shape a second piece of insertion lace A approximately 1/4" from the outside edge of the first lace (**fig. 17**).

19. Join the laces with a featherstitch (L=3.0, W=6.0). Adjust the stitch width as necessary so that the headings of the lace are caught in the stitching (**fig. 17**).

20. Shape a piece of lace edging B approximately 1/4" from the outside edge of the second lace (**fig. 17**).

21. Join the laces with a featherstitch (L=3.0, W=6.0). Adjust the stitch width as necessary so that the headings of the lace are caught in the stitching (**fig. 17**).

22. Soak to remove all traces of the WSS.

23. Starch and press the piece. Lay the piece aside.

24. Repeat steps 2 through 23, creating a second overlay. Be sure that you create a left and right overlay.

25. Place the pieces right sides together (bobbin sides together), matching the edging and pin. Cut two overlays from the pattern, disregarding the previous drawn lines. The outer edge of the lace edging will be placed at the edge of the pattern cutting line.

26. Lay the embellished overlays aside.

Creating the Lower Sleeves

1. Locate the lower sleeve tissue pattern.

2. Fold the tissue in half and draw a vertical line along the crease.

3. Measure over 3-1/4" from the center line and draw a line parallel to the center. Measure over 2" from the second line and draw another line parallel to the center (**fig. 18**).

4. Repeat step 3 on the other side of the center line (**fig. 18**).

5. Trace this pattern with template lines onto a rectangle of silk organza.

6. Center a strip of lace insertion A along the four drawn lines (two on each side of the center). Do not place insertion along the center line (**fig. 19**).

7. Zigzag the lace to the organza along the headings (**refer to fig. 3**).

8. Slit the fabric behind the lace and press away from the lace (**refer to fig. 4**).

9. Zigzag the headings again from the right side (**refer to fig. 5**).

10. From the wrong side, trim the fabric close to the zigzag (**refer to fig. 6**).

11. Pin edging lace C to the organza, matching the scallop of the edging to the center drawn line and the bottom raw edge of the lower sleeve. Miter the lace at the corner. Refer to Basic Heirloom Techniques (found on page 98). Repeat for the other half of the sleeve (**fig. 19**).

12. Zigzag the heading of the lace.

13. Cut the organza along the center drawn line, and just below the lower lace edge, being very careful not to cut the lace.

14. Press the fabric under the lace edging away from the lace (**fig. 20**).

15. Zigzag the heading again from the right side.

16. From the wrong side, trim the fabric close to the zigzag (**fig. 20**).

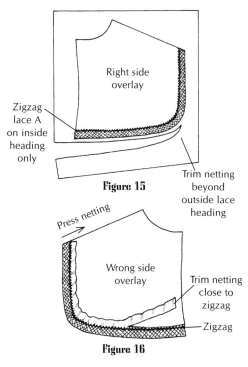

Figure 15

Zigzag lace A on inside heading only

Right side overlay

Trim netting beyond outside lace heading

Press netting

Wrong side overlay

Trim netting close to zigzag

Zigzag

Figure 16

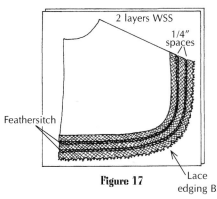

2 layers WSS

1/4" spaces

Featherstitch

Lace edging B

Figure 17

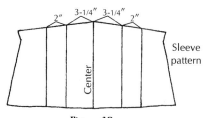

2" 3-1/4" 3-1/4" 2"

Center

Sleeve pattern

Figure 18

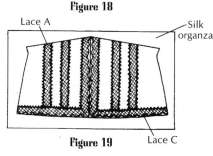

Lace A

Silk organza

Lace C

Figure 19

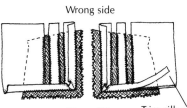

Wrong side

Trim silk organza close to zigzag

Figure 20

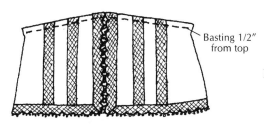

Basting 1/2" from top

Figure 21

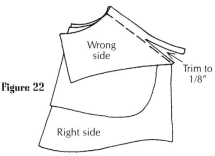

Wrong side

Figure 22

Trim to 1/8"

Right side

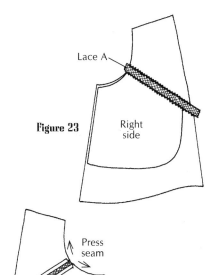

Lace A

Figure 23

Right side

17. Repeat steps 14 through 16 for the remaining portion of the lower sleeve.
18. Place the lower sleeve pieces back onto the tissue pattern and cut along the top cutting line. Machine baste across the top edge to reconnect the two pieces (**fig. 21**).
19. Repeat steps 5 through 18 for the other lower sleeve.
20. Lay the two lower sleeves aside.

Jacket Construction

All seams are 5/8" unless otherwise noted. To finish the seams, trim the seams to 1/4" and overcast the edges by machine or serger.

1. Refer to Jacket General Directions, General Construction, and complete steps 2 through 3 for both sides of the jacket front.
2. Place the jacket upper front to the jacket lower front with right sides together; stitch the seam with a lengthen straight stitch (L=4.0) (**fig. 22**). Loosen the needle tension slightly. This seam will be removed later.
3. Trim the seam allowances between the jacket upper front and jacket lower front to approximately 1/8" (**fig. 22**). Press the seam allowance toward the upper front.
4. Center a strip of Lace A over the seam on the right side of each jacket front.
5. Zigzag the headings of the lace (**fig. 23**).
6. Remove the stitching from the seam and press the fabric under the lace strip toward the upper front and the lower front (**fig. 24**).
7. Zigzag along the lace headings again from the right side (**refer to fig. 23**).
8. Optional: Pinstitch on each side of the lace headings. From the wrong side, trim the fabric close to the zigzag (**fig. 25**).

9. Place the jacket front to the jacket back, right sides together, matching the shoulder and side seams. Stitch and finish the seams; press the seams toward the back.
10. Place the lower sleeve to the upper sleeve, right sides together. Stitch and finish the seam. Press the seam toward the upper sleeve.
11. Place a strip of lace insertion A on the sleeve, placing the lower edge of the insertion along the seam line and mitering the lace at the point (**fig. 26**). Refer to Basic Heirloom Techniques (found on page 98).
12. Zigzag both sides of the lace along the headings (**fig. 26**).
13. Fold the sleeve with right sides together; stitch and finish the seam (**fig. 27**). Press the seam toward the front.
14. Repeat steps 10 through 13 for the remaining sleeve.
15. Refer to the Jacket General Directions, General Construction, Unlined Jacket Version, and complete steps 1 through 9.
16. Cut the length of 1" ribbon in half. Fold under 1/2" on each piece and attach to the jacket front by hand or machine (refer to fig. 22 in the Jacket General Directions).
17. Cut the length of 1/2" ribbon in half. Attach by hand or machine to each sleeve. Tie into a bow (refer to the finished drawing for placement).

Dress Construction

All seams are 5/8" unless otherwise noted. To finish the seams, trim the seams to 1/4" and overcast the edges by machine or serger.

Refer to Dress/Top General Directions and complete all steps.

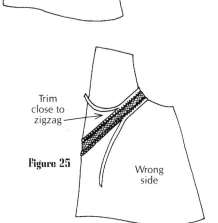

Press seam

Wrong side

Figure 24

Trim close to zigzag

Figure 25

Wrong side

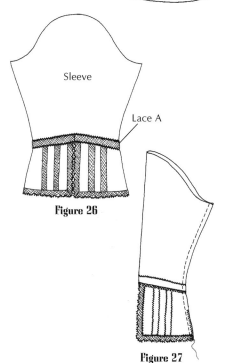

Sleeve

Lace A

Figure 26

Figure 27

Couched Rickrack
Over Blouse and Skirt

Refreshing mint green handkerchief linen is the fabric for this crisp and beautiful top and skirt. The trim around the V'd neckline and the pockets is couched narrow white rickrack stitched in a mint green thread. The couched rickrack is a triple zigzag stitch set to zig and zag in the dips in the rickrack. This is a really cute trim and very elegant on this over blouse. The casings on the pocket are of mint green ribbon and the pockets are gathered with narrow green ribbon. The casing in the back of the over blouse is also green ribbon and once again the narrow ribbon was used to gather in the fullness of the back. The skirt is plain and has a vent opening which is very pretty. This outfit was made by Connie Palmer, a Husqvarna/Viking educator.

This over blouse was made with reference to the Over Blouse General Directions found on page 11.
This skirt was made with reference to the Skirt General Directions with the Open Vent found on page 15.

Supplies

- Refer to the Over Blouse General Directions for fabric requirements
- Refer to Skirt General Directions for fabric requirements
- 1-5/8 yards of 1/4" wide white cotton rickrack for the over blouse
- Decorative thread to coordinate with the linen for the over blouse (we chose a slightly darker color than the linen)
- 1/2" wide silk satin ribbon for the over blouse and pocket casings
    Sizes XS - LG = 1-2/3 yards
    Sizes XL - 4XL = 2 yards
- 1/8" wide silk satin ribbon for the over blouse and pocket ties
    Sizes XS - LG = 3-1/4 yards
    Sizes XL - 4XL = 3-1/2 yards
- Fabric glue
- Thread to match the fabric
- Basic sewing supplies

Pattern Pieces

(located on the pattern tissue)
- Over Blouse Front with V option (curved hem option)
- Over Blouse Front Facing
- Over Blouse Back (curved hem option)
- Over Blouse Back Facing
- Over Blouse Sleeve
- Over Blouse Sleeve Wrist Binding
- Over Blouse Pocket
- Skirt Front
- Skirt Back

Read all instructions for this garment including the referenced General Directions before cutting or constructing the garment.

Cutting and Preparing the Pieces

- Refer to the Over Blouse General Directions, Cutting the Pieces for cutting directions, cutting the over blouse front with the V at the neckline. Omit the over blouse back tie casing, over blouse back ties and over blouse pocket ties; these pieces will be cut from ribbon. Reposition the top casing position line 5/8" from the fold line of the pocket. Mark the center of the pocket between the buttonhole placements on the pattern. You will not need to mark the buttonholes on the pockets. Mark the casing position lines on the over blouse back. Mark the center back between the casing position lines.

- Cut the following from interfacing:
    - One Over Blouse Front Facing on the fold
    - One Over Blouse Back Facing on the fold
- Refer to the Skirt General Directions, Cutting the Pieces for cutting directions.

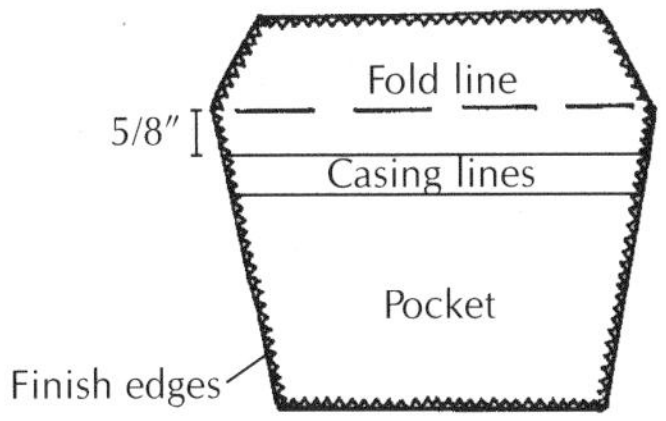

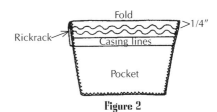

Figure 1

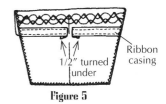

Figure 2

Figure 3

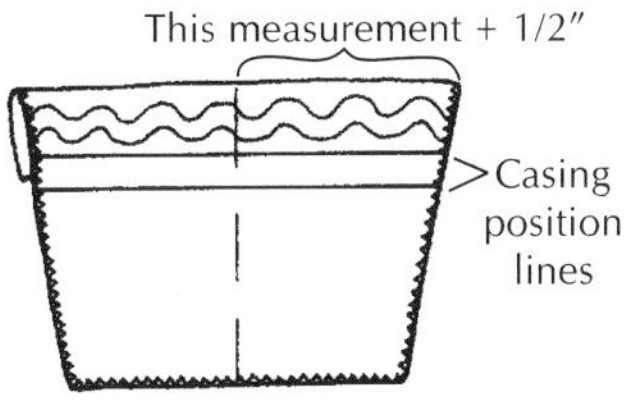

Over Blouse Construction

All seams are 5/8" unless otherwise noted. To finish the seams, trim the seams to 1/4" and overcast the edges by machine or serger.

1. Finish all edges of one pocket with a zigzag or serger (**fig. 1**).
2. Fold under the top edge of the pocket along the fold line and press.
3. Cut a piece of rickrack the width of the pocket and glue baste in place 1/4" from the top folded edge of the pocket (**fig. 2**). Repeat steps 1 through 3 for the remaining pocket.
4. Couch the rickrack in place with a triple zigzag stitch (L=3.5, W=2.5) and the decorative thread. Adjust the zigzag as necessary so the stitch just barely clears the rickrack and hits the fabric in the "valley" of the rickrack (**fig. 3**). Repeat this step for the remaining pocket.
5. Measure from the center mark on the pocket to one side edge of the pocket at the casing position line. Add 1/2" to this measurement (**fig. 4**). Cut four pieces of the 1/2" wide ribbon to this measurement. These will be used for pocket casings.
6. Turn under 1/2" on one end of each of the four ribbon pieces. Center the ribbon casings between the casing position lines on the right side of each pocket with the folded edge of the ribbon at the center mark of the pocket. Straight stitch very close to the edges of the ribbon to create a casing (**fig. 5**).

7. Cut four 11" long pieces of 1/4" ribbon for the ties. With a large safety pin or bodkin, run the ribbon ties through the casings, matching one cut end of the ribbon with the side of the pocket. The other end of the tie will exit the casing at the center of the pocket.
8. Refer to the Over Blouse General Directions, Construction, Pockets and complete steps 7 through 10 and step 12 for both pockets.
9. Measure from the center mark on the jacket back to one side edge of the jacket at the casing position line. Add 1/2" to this measurement (**fig. 6**). Cut two pieces of the 1/2" wide ribbon to this measurement. These will be used for jacket back casings.
10. Turn under 1/2" on one end of each of the ribbon pieces. Center the ribbon casings between the casing position lines on the jacket back with the folded edge of the ribbon at the center mark of the jacket back. Straight stitch very close to the edges of the ribbon to create a casing (**fig. 7**).
11. Cut two one-yard pieces of 1/4" ribbon for the ties. With a large safety pin or bodkin, run the ribbon ties through the casings, matching one cut end of the ribbon with the side of the jacket. The other end of the tie will exit the casing at the center of the jacket back

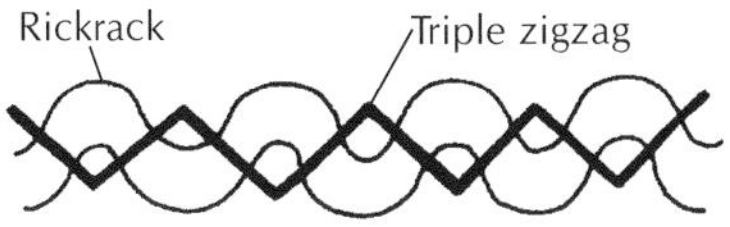

Figure 4

Figure 5

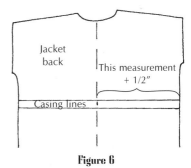

Figure 6

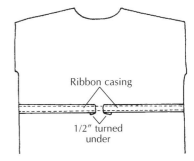

Figure 7

12. Refer to the Over Blouse General Directions, Construction, steps 1 through 6 and complete the steps.

13. With right sides together, match the edge of the sleeve binding, the underarm seam and the bottom of the over blouse. Stitch the sleeve and side seams of the over blouse, beginning at the sleeve binding and stopping at the bottom side edge of the over blouse. The vent is omitted from this over blouse; refer to figure 8.

14. Finish the lower edge of the front and back with a zigzag or serge (**fig. 8**).

15. Turn up a 3/8" hem along the lower edge of the over blouse and pin in place; refer to figure 9.

16. Stitch the hem in place 1/4" from the fold (**fig. 9**).

17. Refer to the Over Blouse General Directions, Construction, steps 20 through 22 and complete the steps.

18. Beginning at one shoulder seam, glue baste the rickrack 1/2" from the finished neck edge (**fig. 10**). Turn under the end of the rickrack and overlap the beginning slightly.

19. Couch the rickrack in place with a triple zigzag stitch (L=3.5, W=2.5), using the decorative thread. Adjust the zigzag as necessary so the stitch just barely clears the rickrack and hits the fabric in the "valley" of the rickrack; refer to figure 3.

Skirt Construction

All seams are 5/8" unless otherwise noted. To finish the seams, trim the seams to 1/4" and overcast the edges by machine or serger.

1. Refer to the Skirt General Directions and complete all steps with the open vent version. All stitching in the General Directions is completed with lightweight sewing thread to match the linen.

2. Straight stitch around the vent opening to secure (**fig. 11**).

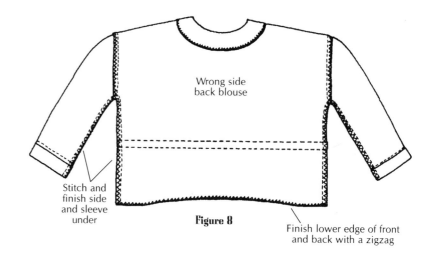

Wrong side back blouse

Stitch and finish side and sleeve under

Finish lower edge of front and back with a zigzag

Figure 8

Blouse back

Blouse front

Stitch in place 5/8" from fold

Figure 9

Turn up 3/8" hem

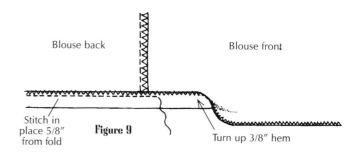

1/2" from neck edge

Rickrack

Figure 10

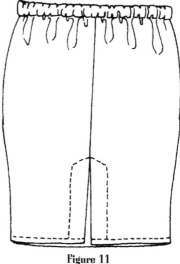

Figure 11

Drawn Thread
Jacket, Top and Skirt

A machine masterpiece has been created by Peggy Dilbone for Husqvarna/Viking. The sage green linen jacket has a beautiful upper bodice with machine drawn thread work, which looks almost identical to hand drawn thread work. The ruffled collar has an edge treatment of triple wing needle entredeux and a crochet edge that looks like tatting on the very edge. The overlay on the jacket is finished on the bottom with a beautiful curved large machine embroidery done in the same sage green tone; gimpwork trails from the top of the overlay down to the machine embroidered scrolls and flowers.

The same gorgeous machine embroidery work is used to finish the sleeves on the bottom part of the sleeve. Peggy used a satin edge to finish the bottom of the portion of the overlay and the sleeves not stitched with the machine embroidery. More decorative pin stitching is found on the plain turned back hem around the bottom of the jacket and the top at the neckline and the bottom. The pin stitch has been used to hem the neckline of the top, the sleeves of the top and the bottom of the jacket.

The skirt has three rows of the wide machine drawn thread work. The hem of the skirt is caught in the stitching of the bottom row of drawn thread work. The skirt has a lapped vent and elastic around the waistline.

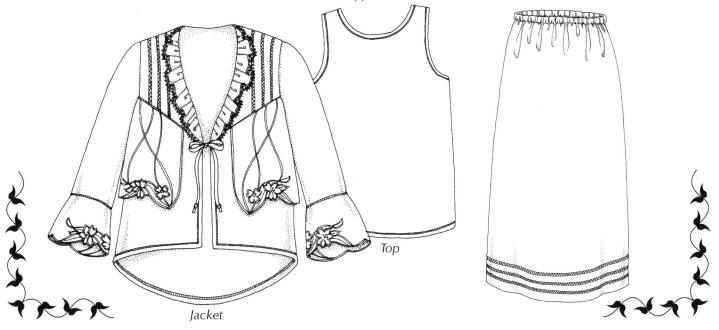

Jacket

Top

This jacket was made with reference to the Jacket General Directions found on page 7.
This top was made with reference to the Dress/Top General Directions found on page 4.
This skirt was made with reference to the Skirt General Directions with the Lapped Vent found on page 15.

Supplies

- Refer to the Jacket General Directions for fabric requirements and add the yardage for the main fabric and the contrast. The jacket is made entirely from the same fabric.
- Refer to the Skirt General Directions for fabric requirements
- Refer to the Dress/Top General Directions for fabric requirements for the top
- Two spools of Sulky rayon thread to match the fabric

- #110 or #120 universal needle for pinstitching
- Two 1/2" decorative pearl buttons
- Small cord or gimp cord for gimpwork
- Open-toe foot
- Lightweight sewing thread to match the fabric
- Heavyweight water soluble stabilizer (WSS)*
- Machine embroidery designs**
- Basic sewing supplies

*When using water soluble stabilizer, the chosen fabric must be washable. The stabilizer must be removed by immersing the garment in water. Tear-away stabilizer may be used for non washable fabrics.

**This jacket was embroidered using a Viking. The embroidery for the jacket is Husqvarna Viking Embroidery Disk #132, Elegant Edgings. You may use this design or substitute another embroidery of your choice.

Pattern Pieces
- Jacket Upper Front
- Jacket Lower Front
- Jacket Lower Front Overlay
- Jacket Back
- Jacket Side Back
- Jacket Upper Sleeve
- Jacket Lower Sleeve
- Jacket Shoulder to Tie Neck Ruffle
- Skirt Front
- Skirt Back
- Dress/Top Front
- Dress/Top Back

Template
(located on the tissue pattern)
- Curve for Ruffle Front

Read all instructions for this garment including the referenced General Directions before cutting or constructing the garment.

Cutting and Preparing the Pieces
- Refer to the layout guide and cut the following pieces for the jacket from the linen fabric:
- Two jacket lower fronts
- One jacket back on the fold
- Two jacket side backs
- Two jacket upper sleeves
- Two rectangles slightly larger than the jacket lower sleeve
- Two rectangles slightly larger than the jacket upper front cut on grain
- Two rectangles slightly larger than the jacket lower front overlay
- Two rectangles slightly larger than the neck ruffle
- Bias strips 1-3/4" wide to go around the neckline and for making the turned cord ties

Refer to the Dress/Top General Directions, Cutting and Preparing the Pieces and follow the steps given for cutting along the line designated for the top.

Refer to the Skirt General Directions, Cutting the Pieces and follow the steps given. Read the directions for the Skirt Construction below before cutting out the skirt.

Jacket

Embellishing the Jacket Front Overlays and Lower Sleeves
1. Trace the overlays and lower sleeves onto the rectangles. Do not cut out.
2. Print out the full sized embroidery design from your computer or copy the full sized template from the book included with the disk. If a full sized copy is not available, refer to Creating a Machine Embroidery Template (found on page 99) and create a template for determining embroidery placement on the garment.
3. Lay the copy or template on the drawn overlay with the edge of the design approximately 3/8" from the lower edge of the overlay. Mark the horizontal and vertical center lines for the embroidery placement.
4. Using two layers of WSS, hoop the overlay fabric and embroider the design (**fig. 1**), trimming the fabric when the embroidery prompts you to do so. If no prompt is given, trim the fabric very close to the lower edge of the embroidery when the embroidery is complete.
5. To finish the edges of the overlay, zigzag (L=1.0, W=2.0) with an open-toe foot along the drawn line (**fig. 2**). Trim the fabric close to the zigzag. Place WSS beneath the zigzag and then satin stitch over the cut edge.
6. Repeat steps 3 through 5, mirror imaging the design for the opposite overlay.
7. Rinse the fabric to completely remove any traces of WSS.
8. Place the embroidered overlay pieces right sides together matching the embroideries.
9. Cut out the overlays using the overlay pattern piece (**fig. 3**).
10. Draw several curvy lines for the gimpwork on the overlays. The lines are random and do not have to match (**fig. 3**).
11. Refer to Gimpwork (found on page 102) and complete the gimpwork along the drawn lines.
12. Refer to the steps above and embroider (**fig. 4**) and cut out (**fig. 5**) the two lower sleeves

Figure 1

Figure 2

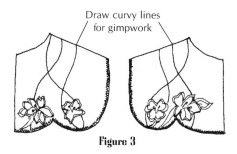

Draw curvy lines for gimpwork

Figure 3

Figure 4

Figure 5

Martha's Fabulous Fashions

omitting the gimpwork lines that were stitched on the overlays. Rinse away the stabilizer and allow the pieces to dry.

13. Starch and press the overlays and lower sleeves and lay aside.

Embellishing the Jacket Upper Front

1. Cut a tissue pattern of the jacket upper front in the chosen size (**fig. 6**).

2. Pull a vertical thread in the center of one of the upper front blocks (**fig. 7**).

3. Draw out 1/4" of threads vertically on the block alternating from one side to the other of the thread pulled in step 2. This will give a 1/4" wide "run" in the fabric (**fig. 8**).

4. Measure over 1" from each outside edge of the "run" and pull another thread (**fig. 8**).

5. Continue drawing out threads to create three 1/4" wide runs 1" apart (**fig. 9**).

6. Starch and press the blocks.

7. Thread the machine with rayon thread in the needle and lightweight thread in the bobbin.

8. Choose a pinstitch (L=3.5, W=2.0) and an open toe foot. Position a "run" under the machine foot. The center of the foot should be on the first thread next to the "run". The fingers of the stitch are toward the fabric. The straight part of the stitch is on the drawn thread area.

9. Stitch down both sides of the "run" bundling the threads (**fig. 10**).

10. Repeat steps 2 through 9 for the other upper front block.

11. Starch and press the blocks well. Place the blocks right sides together aligning the hemstitched areas.

12. Cut two upper fronts using the tissue pattern (**fig. 11**). Lay the pieces aside.

Embellishing the Ruffle

1. Trace the neck ruffle onto the two fabric rectangles. Using the template, trace the curve for the ruffle front on each rectangle (**fig. 12**).

2. Place WSS under the ruffle. Choose a triple entredeux stitch on the machine. Stitch the entredeux stitch 3/8" from the raw edge of the fabric following the drawn curve of the ruffle (**fig. 12**).

3. When the stitch is complete, trim the seam allowance close to the stitching (**fig. 13**).

4. Optional: Place WSS under the ruffle and stitch a crochet edge with Sulky rayon thread in the needle and the bobbin. Stitch around the collar so the stitch catches the decorative edge, but the scallop of the stitch goes onto the WSS (**fig. 14**). Cut away the excess WSS.

5. Rinse the fabric to remove all traces of WSS.

6. Repeat steps 1 through 4 for the other neck ruffle. Lay the ruffle pieces aside.

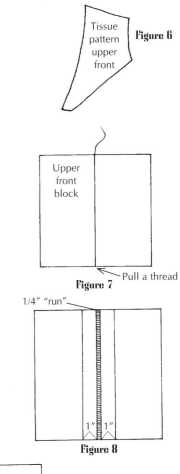

Tissue pattern upper front **Figure 6**

Upper front block

Pull a thread

Figure 7

1/4" "run"

1" 1"

Figure 8

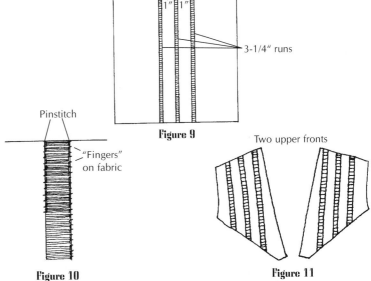

1" 1"

3-1/4" runs

Figure 9

Pinstitch

"Fingers" on fabric

Figure 10

Two upper fronts

Figure 11

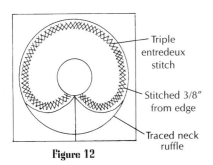

Triple entredeux stitch

Stitched 3/8" from edge

Traced neck ruffle

Figure 12

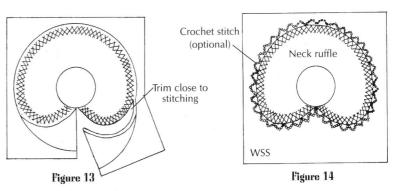

Trim close to stitching

Figure 13

Crochet stitch (optional)

Neck ruffle

WSS

Figure 14

Jacket Construction

All seams are 5/8" unless otherwise noted. To finish the seams, trim the seams to 1/4" and overcast the edges by machine or serger.

1. Refer to the Jacket General Directions, General Construction and complete steps 2 through 4 for both jacket fronts and steps 6 and 7 for the jacket back.

2. Place the jacket front to the jacket back, right sides together, matching the shoulder and side seams. Stitch and finish the shoulder seams. Stitch and finish the side seams stopping approximately 6" from the lower edge. Clip through the seam allowance at the stopping point (**fig. 15**).

3. Refer to the Jacket General Directions, General Construction and complete step 12. Pinstitch close to the seam on the lower sleeves (**fig. 16**) and then complete step 13.

4. Stitch the bias strips together to make one continuous length of bias (**fig. 17**). Fold the bias in half and press being careful not to stretch the bias (**fig. 18**).

5. Pin the wrong side of the neck ruffle to the right side of the jacket from the shoulder seam to the center front neckline. Stitch the ruffle to the jacket 1/2" from the raw edges (**fig. 19**). Clip through the jacket seam allowance at each tapered end of the neck ruffle. This will allow the bias facing to be turned back while the jacket front remains extended. The ruffle and the jacket will now be treated as one.

6. Pin the folded bias to the jacket neck edge beginning and ending at the clips (**fig. 20**).

7. Stitch the bias to the jacket with a 5/8" seam (**fig. 20**). Trim the seam to 1/4". Turn under the ends of the bias and turn the bias completely to the inside of the jacket and whip stitch in place (**fig. 21**). The jacket fronts will be extended.

8. Finish the front edges of the jacket, the bottom edges of the jacket front and back and both sides of the vent openings on each side with a zigzag or serge.

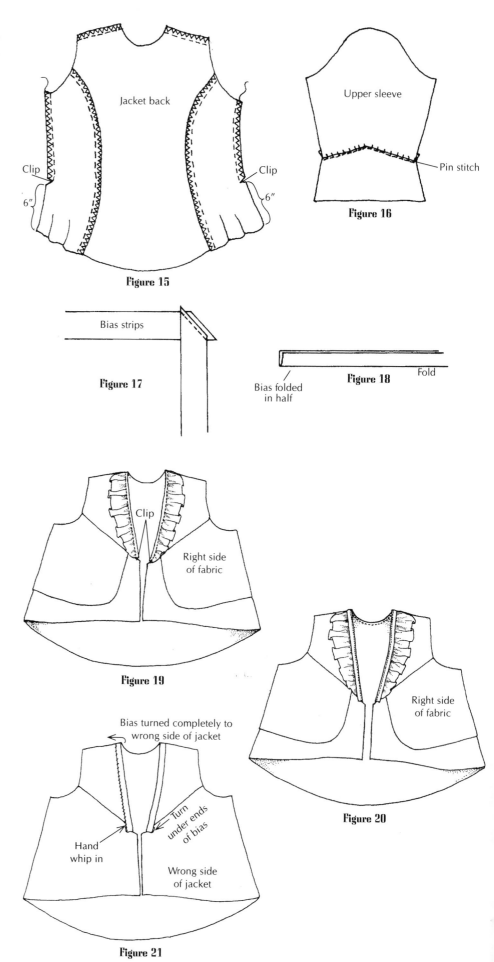

Figure 15

Figure 16

Figure 17

Figure 18

Figure 19

Figure 20

Figure 21

9. Press the finished edges at 5/8" to the wrong side of the jacket (**fig. 22**).

10. From the right side of the jacket, pinstitch (L=3.0, W=2.0) along the inside edge of the hem letting the fingers of the pinstitch catch the hem. Pinstitch the jacket front edges, the hem on the jacket front and back and both sides of the vents (**fig. 23**).

11. Stitch a row of lengthened machine stitching between the notches on the sleeve cap for easing (**fig. 24**). Pin the sleeves into the armholes, matching the side seams of the jacket to the sleeve seams. Stitch and finish the seams (**fig. 25**). Press the seams toward the sleeves.

12. Cut two strips of unpieced bias 24" long. Refer to the technique, Creating a Turned Cord (found on page 100) and create two cords for the jacket ties.

13. Attach the ties on the wrong side of the jacket at the center front (refer to fig. 22 in the Jacket General Directions for placement). A pearl button is added on each side at the center front.

Top Construction

All seams are 5/8" unless otherwise noted. To finish the seams, trim the seams to 1/4" and overcast the edges by machine or serger.

1. Refer to the Dress/Top General Directions and complete all steps.

2. When construction is complete, pinstitch around the neckline and armhole openings positioning the fingers of the stitch to catch the bias and the straight part of the stitch to fall on the single layer fabric (**fig. 26**).

3. Pinstitch the hem of the top positioning the fingers of the stitch to catch the hem and the straight part of the stitch to fall on the single layer fabric (**fig. 26**).

Skirt Construction

All seams are 5/8" unless otherwise noted. To finish the seams, trim the seams to 1/4" and overcast the edges by machine or serger.

1. The bottom edge of the skirt must be on straight of grain. Before cutting the skirt, pull a thread in the linen and place the bottom edge of the pattern pieces along the pulled thread (**fig. 27**).

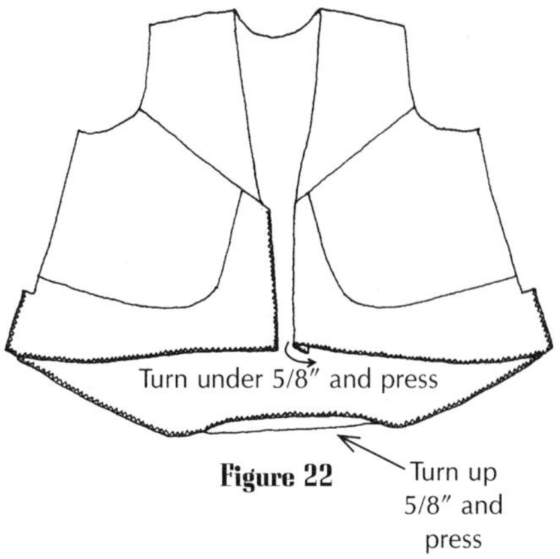

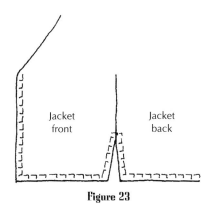

Turn under 5/8" and press

Figure 22

Turn up 5/8" and press

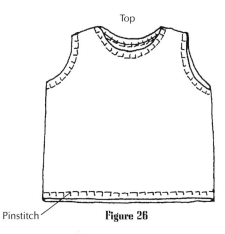

Jacket front

Jacket back

Figure 23

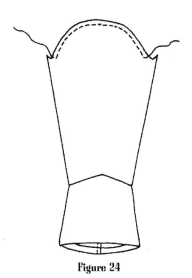

Figure 24

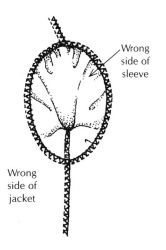

Wrong side of sleeve

Wrong side of jacket

Figure 25

Top

Pinstitch

Figure 26

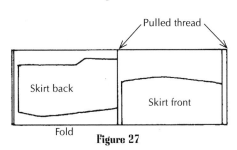

Pulled thread

Skirt back

Skirt front

Fold

Figure 27

2. Measure 3-1/2" from the bottom edge of the skirt front and backs and mark a line (**fig. 28**).

3. Mark two more lines 1-1/4" above this line (**fig. 28**).

4. Draw out the threads for 1/4" starting on each of these lines and working up the skirt (**fig. 29**).

5. Finish the sides of the skirt front and the sides of the skirt back with a zigzag or serge (**fig. 29**). Place the skirt front to the skirt backs, right sides together and stitch the side seams (**fig. 30**). Press the seams open (**fig. 31**).

6. Finish the bottom edge of the skirt front and backs with a zigzag or serge (**fig. 32**).

7. Press the hem up so it meets the first line of the drawn thread area. Baste the hem in place (**fig. 33**).

8. Pinstitch (L-4.0, W-2.5) using an open toe foot or clear foot. The fingers of the stitch should catch the hem and the straight part of the stitch is on the drawn thread area (**fig. 34**). Stitch with Sulky rayon thread in the needle and lightweight thread in the bobbin.

9. Stitch down both sides of the drawn areas bundling the threads (**refer to fig. 10**).

10. Starch and press the pieces.

11. Refer to the Skirt General Directions and complete steps 1 through 3 Lapped Vent Version.

12. Refer to the Skirt General Directions and complete steps 5 through 7 and steps 10 through 12.

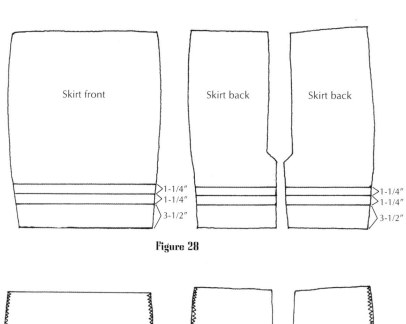

Figure 28

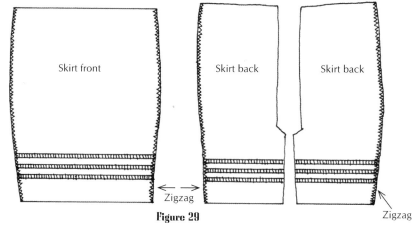

Figure 29

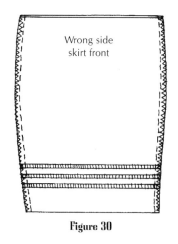

Figure 30

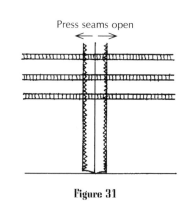

Figure 31

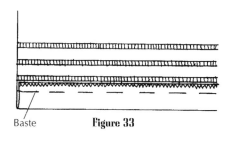

Figure 32

Figure 33

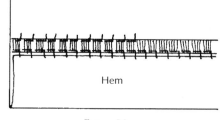

Figure 34

Embroidered Lace and Linen Over Blouse and Skirt

Fresher than a spring day is this beautiful mint green handkerchief linen skirt and over blouse. There are so many details to truly enjoy making this outfit. The pockets are made of antique lace insertion in ecru; the top of the pocket has French lace beading with ribbon run through the beading and a narrow silk organza band at the top. The pocket has been pinstitched to the dress and the organza top is pinstitched to the top of the French lace beading. There is the most beautiful ecru corded machine embroidery which goes around the neckline. Silk organza bands are found at the bottom of the sleeves and at the bottom of the skirt. Three absolutely fabulous machine embroidery designs are found on the neckline, one on each sleeve and four on the skirt front and back. The silk organza bands are joined to the bottom of the sleeves and the bottom of the skirt with the same white French antiqué lace insertion which is used for the pockets. The lace, once again, has been pinstitched to the fabric.

The machine embroidery design is an Urban Zündt design from the CD Zündt Designs I exclusively for Martha Pullen Company. The design has leaves and lily of the valley flowers. The colors of the embroidery design are blue, tan, green and white. The skirt has a lapped vent in the back and has elastic at the waistline. The skirt and top were made by Sue Pennington Stewart.

This over blouse was made with reference to the Over blouse General Directions found on page 11.
This skirt was made with reference to the Skirt General Directions with the Lapped Vent found on page 15.

Supplies

- Refer to the Over Blouse General Directions for fabric and interfacing requirements
- Refer to the Skirt General Directions for fabric requirements
- 2/3 yard of organza for hemline of the skirt, the bottom edge of the sleeves and the pocket embellishments
- 10 yards of 5/8″ wide lace insertion (NOTE: The over blouse pictured was made using the same lace pattern on the pockets. If you wish to use two different lace patterns, purchase 3-1/4 yards of a different lace pattern and subtract 3-1/4 yards from the amount given above)

- 2 yards of 5/8″ beading for over blouse pocket and back casings
- 3-1/3 yards of 1/4″ ribbon for over blouse pocket and back ties
- Gimp cord or #12 pearl cotton for the corded entredeux stitch
- Tear-away stabilizer
- #100 or #110 universal needle for stitching the entredeux stitch
- Four 8″ squares of heavyweight water soluble stabilizer (WSS)
- Lightweight sewing thread to match the fabric and lace
- Sulky 40 wt. decorative rayon thread in colors to compliment the chosen fabric
- Lace shaping board

- KK 2000 (temporary spray adhesive)
- Machine embroidery designs*
- Basic sewing supplies

*The embroidery for the over blouse and skirt pictured is from Zündt Designs, Volume I, by Martha Pullen, Corner Bow With Flowers. You may use this embroidery or substitute another embroidery design which measure approximately 3-1/4″ wide by 4-3/4″ high.

Pattern Pieces

(located on the pattern tissue)

- Over Blouse Front with V option (curved hem option)
- Over Blouse Front Facing
- Over Blouse Back (curved hem option)
- Over Blouse Back Facing
- Over Blouse Sleeve
- Over Blouse Pocket
- Over Blouse Back Tie Casing
- Over Blouse Back Tie
- Over Blouse Pocket Tie
- Skirt Front
- Skirt Back

Templates

(located on the tissue pattern)

- Sleeve Scallop Template
- Skirt Front and Back Scallop Template

Read all instructions for this garment including the referenced General Directions before cutting or constructing the garment.

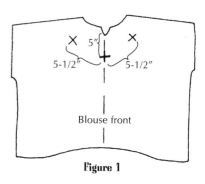

Figure 1

Cutting and Preparing the Pieces

- Refer to the Over Blouse General Directions, Cutting the Pieces for cutting directions, omitting the over blouse sleeve wrist binding. The over blouse front, over blouse back and sleeves are cut from the main over blouse fabric. The over blouse back casing and the pockets are made from lace (instructions included below). The back ties and pocket ties are ribbon.
- Cut the following from interfacing:
  - One Over Blouse Front Facing on the fold
  - One Over Blouse Back Facing on the fold

- Refer to the Skirt General Directions, Cutting the Pieces for cutting directions. Mark the back vent fold line on both skirt back pieces.
- From the organza cut the following:
  - Two pieces 6" by the width of the lower edge of the over blouse sleeve pattern
  - Two pieces 2-1/2 " by 12" for the pockets
  - One piece 8" by the width of the lower skirt front
  - Two pieces 8" by the width of the lower skirt back

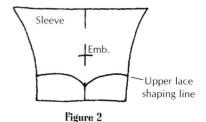

Figure 2

Over Blouse Construction

All seams are 5/8" unless otherwise noted. To finish the seams, trim the seams to 1/4" and overcast the edges by machine or serger.

1. Refer to the technique Creating a Machine Embroidery Template (found on page 99) and stitch a template onto a scrap of organza. Re-mark the center of the embroidery on the template.
2. Position the template approximately 5" below the point of the V on the over blouse front. Mark the center. Position the embroidery template on each side of the center approximately 5" below the neck edge. The centers of the side embroideries should be approximately 5-1/2" from the center embroidery. Mark the centers for the embroideries (**fig. 1**).
3. Fold each sleeve in half and mark the vertical center. Place the sleeve scallop template line marked "place raw edge of sleeve here to trace template" along the

lower edge of each sleeve. Trace the upper lace shaping line and mark the center for the embroidery (**fig. 2**). Repeat this step for the other sleeve.
4. If you would like to complete all embroidery for the over blouse and skirt, complete steps 1 through 3 under Skirt Construction, page 5.
5. Stabilize, hoop and embroider the designs. Remove the stabilizer and press well.
6. Refer to the Over Blouse General Directions and complete steps 1 through 4 (do not finish the lower edge of the facings). Do not tack the facing to the neckline.
7. Draw a line 1-3/4" from the finished over blouse neckline following the shape of the neckline (**fig. 3**).

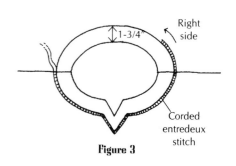

Figure 3

8. Pin the front and back facing to the over blouse.

9. Beginning at a shoulder seam, stitch along the drawn line with a corded entredeux stitch through the over blouse and facing (L=2.5, W=4.0). Refer to the technique, Corded Entredeux (found on page 100) (**fig. 3**).

10. From the wrong side of the over blouse, trim away the excess facing (**fig. 4**).

11. Embellish the lower edge of the sleeves as follows:

    a. Fold one of the 6″ pieces of organza in half to measure 3″. Place the fold of the organza onto the line designated on the sleeve scallop template. Trace both lace shaping lines onto the organza (**fig. 5**).

    b. Refer to the technique Lace Shaping Scallops, found on page 101 and shape the lace onto the organza.

    c. Stitch the lace heading to the organza along the lower lace shaping line only. Trim away the excess organza from behind the lace (**fig. 6**). Stitch the miter (**fig. 7**).

    d. Place the organza/lace band on the bottom edge of the sleeve, aligning the top edge of the lace to the upper lace shaping line drawn on the sleeve. The fold of the organza will be approximately 5/8″ above the raw edge of the sleeve. Be sure that the sleeve embroidery is in line with the center of the template (**fig. 8**).

    e. Stitch the upper lace shaping line to attach the organza/lace band to the sleeve. Trim away the excess fabric from behind the lace (**fig. 9**).

    f. Repeat the steps above for the other sleeve.

12. Complete two pockets as follows; use fabric glue or KK2000 to adhere the lace to the WSS:

    a. Trace the pocket pattern onto a square of WSS stabilizer. Mark the side and bottom stitching lines of the pocket 5/8″ from each edge. Draw a line along the vertical center of the pocket (**refer to fig. 10**).

    b. Beginning along one side of the pocket, place a strip of lace insertion even with the marked stitching line. The ends of the lace should extend 1/4″ above the lower casing line drawn on the WSS and 1/4″ below the bottom stitching line (**fig. 10**).

    c. Continue adding lace until one half of the drawn pocket is covered. When the lace begins to cross the center drawn line, cut the lace 1/4″ beyond the center line (**fig. 11**).

    d. Repeat steps a though c on another piece of WSS creating a mirror image side of the lace pocket.

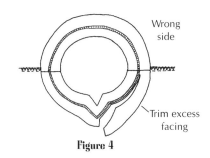

Figure 4

Wrong side

Trim excess facing

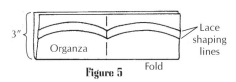

Figure 5

3″ Organza Lace shaping lines Fold

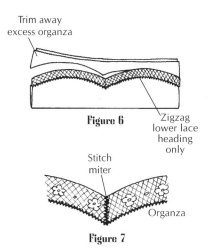

Trim away excess organza

Figure 6

Zigzag lower lace heading only

Stitch miter

Figure 7

Organza

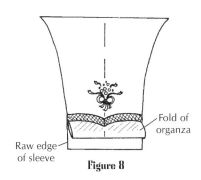

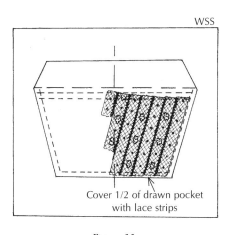

Fold of organza

Raw edge of sleeve

Figure 8

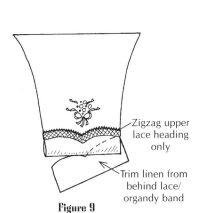

Zigzag upper lace heading only

Trim linen from behind lace/ organdy band

Figure 9

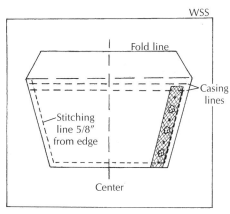

WSS

Fold line

Casing lines

Stitching line 5/8″ from edge

Center

Figure 10

WSS

Cover 1/2 of drawn pocket with lace strips

Figure 11

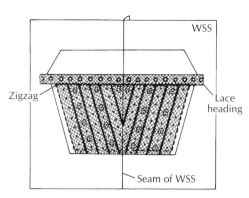

Figure 12

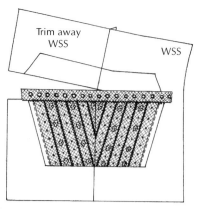

Figure 13

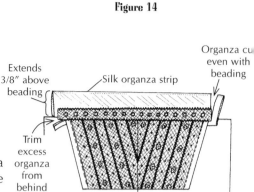

Figure 14

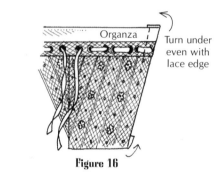

Figure 15

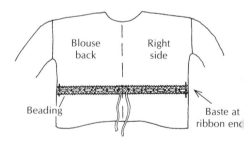

Figure 16

e. Stitch the laces together through the WSS with a narrow zigzag (**fig. 11**).

f. Place the two mirror image lace shapes right sides together, matching the laces and the center line. Straight stitch the two pieces together along the vertical center of the pocket. Trim the seam to a scant 1/4″ and finish the seam with a zigzag.

g. Place the pocket with the WSS still attached right side up on a lace shaping board (**refer to fig. 12**).

h. Place a strip of lace beading across the top of the pocket, aligning the lower edge of the lace beading to the lower casing line. The beading should extend 1/4″ beyond each side of the pocket. Stitch the beading to the lace pocket, with a narrow lengthened zigzag along the lower casing line (**fig. 12**). Trim the excess lace ends and the upper portion of the WSS from behind the beading (**fig. 13**).

i. Fold the organza strip for the pocket in half to measure 1-1/4″ (**fig. 14**) and place it behind the lace beading. The fold of the organza should be at the top and extend approximately 3/8″ above the lace beading (**fig. 15**). Zigzag across both edges of the lace beading to secure the organza behind the beading; this creates the casing. Trim the excess organza from behind the lace pocket.

j. Cut the ends of the organza even with the ends of the beading (**fig. 15**).

k. Rinse away the WSS from the pocket. Let dry and press well.

l. Cut two 11″ pieces of 1/4″ ribbon. With a medium safety pin or a bodkin, run the ribbon through the casing; place one end of the ribbon even with the cut end of the beading. The other end will exit a beading hole at the center of the pocket (**fig. 16**).

m. Turn under the bottom edge of the pocket 1/4″ and press. Turn under the ends of the organza/beading even with the edge of the lace pocket (**fig. 16**).

13. Refer to the Over Blouse General Directions, Pockets and complete steps 8 through 10 and step 12 for both pockets. Complete step 5 in the Over Blouse General Directions to insert the sleeves.

14. Place a length of beading across the over blouse back between the casing position lines. Stitch the beading to the over blouse back along each heading with a narrow zigzag.

15. Cut two pieces of 1/4″ ribbon the same length as the over blouse back tie pattern for the chosen size.

16. Weave the ribbon through the beading as you did for the sleeves. The ribbons will exit at the center back of the over blouse. Baste the ends of the ribbon to the sides of the over blouse (**fig. 17**).

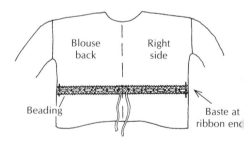

Figure 17

17. With right sides together, match the front to the back at the edge of the sleeve organza, the underarm seam and the bottom edge of the over blouse. Stitch the sleeve and side seams of the over blouse, beginning at the sleeve binding and stopping at the notch just below the back casing. Backstitch

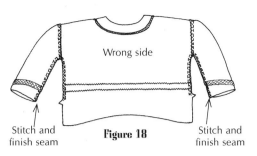

Stitch and finish seam

Wrong side

Figure 18

Stitch and finish seam

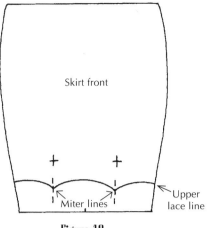

Skirt front

Miter lines

Upper lace line

Figure 19

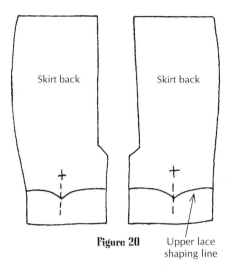

Skirt back

Skirt back

Figure 20

Upper lace shaping line

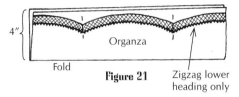

4"

Organza

Fold

Figure 21

Zigzag lower heading only

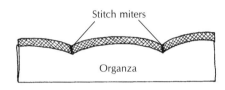

Stitch miters

Organza

Figure 22

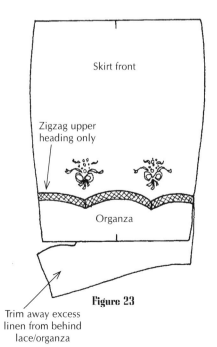

Skirt front

Zigzag upper heading only

Organza

Figure 23

Trim away excess linen from behind lace/organza

at the notch and across the casing to secure. Finish the seam (**fig. 18**).

18. Refer to the Over Blouse General Directions and complete steps 14 through 19 and step 22.

Skirt Construction

All seams are 5/8" unless otherwise noted. To finish the seams, trim the seams to 1/4" and overcast the edges by machine or serger.

1. Place the skirt front scallop template onto the lower raw edge of the skirt front along the designated line and align the template at the center front of the skirt. Trace the upper lace shaping line and miter lines; mark the center for the embroideries. Adjust the embroidery placement as needed. Flip the template and trace the same on the other side of the skirt front (**fig. 19**).

2. Place the skirt back scallop template onto the lower edge of the skirt backs, along the designated line. Align the designated line of the template to the back vent fold line on the skirt back. Trace the upper lace shaping line and mark the centers for the embroideries (**fig. 20**).

3. Stabilize, hoop and embroider the lower portion of the skirt. There will be four embroideries on all sizes.

4. Embellish the lower edge of the skirt as follows:

   a. Fold the 8" piece of organza for the skirt front in half to measure 4". Place the fold of the organza onto the line designated on the skirt front scallop template. Trace the lace shaping lines and miters onto the organza.

   b. Refer to the technique Lace Shaping Scallops (found on page 101) and shape the lace onto the organza.

   c. Remove from the template and stitch the lace to the organza along the lower lace shaping line only (**fig. 21**). Trim away the excess organza from behind the lace. Stitch the miters (**fig. 22**).

   d. Place the organza/lace band on the bottom edge of the skirt front, aligning the top edge of the lace to the template line transferred to the skirt front. Be sure that the skirt embroidery is in line with the lace miters.

   e. Stitch along the upper lace shaping line to attach the organza/lace band to the skirt front. Trim away the excess skirt fabric from behind the lace (**fig. 23**).

   f. Repeat the steps a through e above for the skirt backs, using the skirt back scallop template.

   g. Trim away the excess organza/lace band even with the side edge of the skirt front and backs and even with the inside edge of the vent if necessary.

5. Refer to the Skirt General Directions and complete steps 1 through 7 (choosing the lapped vent version and steps 10 through 12.

Embroidered Organza Over Blouse and Skirt

Absolutely perfect, very fashionable and so very young looking are these two pieces. I love the way Pam Mahshie used three different mediums in a very similar shade of blue--blue linen, blue silk organza and blue machine embroidery. The neckline of the pale blue cotton linen blend over blouse has the V'd option. The sleeves are long. There is a blue organza band at the bottom of both the over blouse and skirt. The over blouse and skirt were shortened before adding the four-inch organza band. There is a large continual machine embroidery design all the way around the top and skirt; the color is once again blue. The skirt has elastic and has a lapped vent in the back. This cute outfit was made by Pam Mahshie of Babylock.

This over blouse was made with reference to the Over Blouse General Directions found on page 11.
This skirt was made with reference to the Skirt General Directions with the Lapped Vent found on page 15.

Supplies

- Refer to the Over Blouse General Directions for fabric and interfacing requirements
- Refer to the Skirt General Directions for fabric requirements
- One yard of organza for hemline of the over blouse and skirt.
- Medium to heavyweight water soluble stabilizer (WSS)*
- Thread to match the fabric and lace
- 40 wt. decorative rayon thread to coordinate with the chosen fabric
- Machine embroidery designs**
- Basic sewing supplies

*Water soluble stabilizer is the recommended stabilizer when sewing on sheer fabrics; however, the chosen fabrics must be washable. The stabilizer must be removed by emersing the garment in water.

**This over blouse and skirt were embroidered using a Babylock Ellageo. The embroidery for the over blouse and skirt is from The Amazing Designer series Jessica McClintock. You may use this embroidery or substitute another embroidery which measures approximately 4" high.

Pattern Pieces

(located on the pattern tissue)

- Over Blouse Front with the V option and straight hemline option (shorten the over blouse front 8-1/4" from the lower cut edge of the over blouse)
- Over Blouse Front Facing
- Over Blouse Back with straight hemline option (shorten the over blouse back 8-1/4" from the lower cut edge of the over blouse)
- Over Blouse Back Facing
- Over Blouse Sleeve
- Over Blouse Sleeve Wrist Binding
- Skirt Front (shorten pattern 4-1/4")
- Skirt Back (shorten pattern 4-1/4")